3

INSIDE WRITING

The Academic Word List in Context

Kate Adams

SERIES DIRECTOR:

Cheryl Boyd Zimmerman

OXFORD

UNIVERSITY PRESS

198 Madison Avenue
New York, NY 10016 USA

Great Clarendon Street, Oxford, OX2 6DP, United Kingdom

Oxford University Press is a department of the University of Oxford.
It furthers the University's objective of excellence in research, scholarship,
and education by publishing worldwide. Oxford is a registered trade
mark of Oxford University Press in the UK and in certain other countries

Director, ELT New York: Laura Pearson
Head of Adult, ELT New York: Stephanie Karras
Development Editor: Rebecca Meyer
Executive Art and Design Manager: Maj-Britt Hagsted
Content Production Manager: Julie Armstrong
Design Project Manager: Michael Steinhofer
Image Manager: Trisha Masterson
Production Artist: Julie Sussman Perez
Production Coordinator: Christopher Espejo

ISBN: 978 0 19 460136 8

Printed in China

This book is printed on paper from certified and well-managed sources

ACKNOWLEDGEMENTS

Illustrations by: 5W Infographics, pgs. 16, 28.

*We would also like to thank the following for permission to reproduce the following
photographs:* **Cover**, Joson/Corbis; Sven Tideman/Nordicphotos/Corbis; Radius
Images/Corbis; Murat Taner/Corbis; Imagemore Co., Ltd./Imagemore Co.,
Ltd./Corbis; Thierry Dosogne / Getty Images; Masterfile; Jennifer Gottschalk/
shutterstock. **Interior**, p1 VLADJ55/shutterstock; p2 Gavin Hellier/Alamy; p15
iofoto/shutterstock; p31 DSGpro/Getty Images; p32 Fascinations; p33 Bio Brite
Inc. (bio brite); p33 Matthias Lange (matthias); p45 karamysh/shutterstock;
p47 Reza Estakhrian/Getty Images; p61 SeDmi/shutterstock; p62 c.Warner Br/
Everett/Rex Features; p63 Herbert Kratky/shutterstock; p64 Stephen Frink
Collection/Alamy; p77 han871111/shutterstock; p78 EuroStyle Graphics/
Alamy; p89 Anna Stowe/Alamy; p93 Roman Gorielov/Fotolia; p94 OJO Images
Ltd/Alamy; p95 Jake Curtis/Getty Images; p96 Visage/Getty Images; p109
Peshkova/shutterstock; p110 John O'Gready/The Sydney Morning Herald/
Fairfax Media/Getty Images (man on wire); p110 Ronald Grant Archive (close-
up man); p111 Robert Kneschke/Fotolia; p125 STILLFX/shutterstock; p126
Steve Oehlenschlager/shutterstock; p127 – 128, Wayzgoose, Inc.; p141 Kim
Westerskov/Getty Images; p142 Grant Faint/Oxford University Press; p143
Prisma Bildagentur AG/Alamy; p144 YAY Media AS/Alamy; p153 2011 Gamma-
Rapho/Getty Images.

Acknowledgements

We would like to acknowledge the following individuals for their input during the development of the series:

Salam Affouneh
Higher Colleges of Technology
Abu Dhabi, U.A.E.

Kristin Bouton
Intensive English Institute
Illinois, U.S.A.

Nicole H. Carrasquel
Center for Multilingual Multicultural Studies
Florida, U.S.A.

Elaine Cockerham
Higher College of Technology
Muscat, Oman

Danielle Dilkes
CultureWorks English as a Second Language Inc.
Ontario, Canada

Susan Donaldson
Tacoma Community College
Washington, U.S.A

Penelope Doyle
Higher Colleges of Technology
Dubai, U.A.E.

Edward Roland Gray
Yonsei University
Seoul, South Korea

Melanie Golbert
Higher Colleges of Technology
Abu Dhabi, U.A.E.

Elise Harbin
Alabama Language Institute
Alabama, U.S.A.

Bill Hodges
University of Guelph
Ontario, Canada

David Daniel Howard
National Chiayi University
Chiayi

Leander Hughes
Saitama Daigaku
Saitama, Japan

James Ishler
Higher Colleges of Technology
Fujairah, U.A.E.

John Iveson
Sheridan College
Ontario, Canada

Alan Lanes
Higher Colleges of Technology
Dubai, U.A.E.

Corinne Marshall
Fanshawe College
Ontario, Canada

Christine Matta
College of DuPage
Illinois, U.S.A.

Beth Montag
University at Kearney
Nebraska, U.S.A.

Kevin Mueller
Tokyo International University
Saitama, Japan

Tracy Anne Munteanu
Higher Colleges of Technology
Fujairah, U.A.E.

Eileen O'Brien
Khalifa University of Science, Technology, and Research
Sharjah, U.A.E.

Jangyo Parsons
Kookmin University
Seoul, South Korea

John P. Racine
Dokkyo Daigaku
Soka City, Japan

Scott Rousseau
American University of Sharjah
Sharjah, U.A.E.

Jane Ryther
American River College
California, U.S.A

Kate Tindle
Zayed University
Dubai, U.A.E.

Melody Traylor
Higher Colleges of Technology
Fujairah, U.A.E.

John Vogels
Higher Colleges of Technology
Dubai, U.A.E.

Kelly Wharton
Fanshawe College
Ontario, Canada

Contents

The Inside Track to Academic Success

Student Books

For additional student resources visit: www.oup.com/elt/insidewriting

iTools for all levels

The *Inside Writing* iTools is for use with an LCD projector or interactive whiteboard.

Resources for whole-class presentation

> **Book-on-screen** focuses class on teaching points and facilitates classroom management.
> **Writing worksheets** provide additional practice with the genre and Writing Models.

Resources for assessment and preparation

> Customizable Unit, Mid-term, and Final Tests evaluate student progress.
> Answer Keys

Additional instructor resources at: www.oup.com/elt/teacher/insidewriting

UNIT 1

Soaring to the Top

In this unit, you will

> analyze an architecture review and learn how it is used to describe a building.
> use descriptive writing.
> increase your understanding of the target academic words for this unit.

WRITING SKILLS

> Descriptive Language
> Spatial Organization
> **GRAMMAR** Passive and Active Voice

Self-Assessment

Think about how well you know each target word, and check (✓) the appropriate column. I have…

TARGET WORDS	never seen the word before.	heard or seen the word but am not sure what it means.	heard or seen the word and understand what it means.	used the word confidently in *either* speaking or writing.
AWL				
abstract				
allocate				
bulk				
🔑 colleague				
comprise				
🔑 cycle				
dynamic				
🔑 estate				
furthermore				
hence				
🔑 logic				
🔑 obtain				
refine				
🔑 transform				

🔑 Oxford 3000™ keywords

Building Knowledge

Read these questions. Discuss your answers in a small group.

1. What buildings do you like? Why do you like them?

2. What makes some spaces more pleasant to be in than others? Why?

3. What information would you expect to find in a review of a building?

Writing Model

An architecture review is a detailed description of a building's features. Read about the Burj Khalifa, a skyscraper in Dubai, U.A.E.

Soaring to the Top: The Burj Khalifa

by Stefano Urankowski

The Burj Khalifa in Dubai has **obtained**, for the moment, the title of the world's tallest building. At 828 meters tall, it towers over other great skyscrapers. It is easily
5 twice as tall as the Empire State Building in New York. In fact, when it was completed in 2009, the Burj Khalifa was over 300 meters taller than the Taipei 101 tower in Taiwan, which had been the world's tallest building.
10   The team of Adrian Smith and William Baker, **colleagues** from the architectural firm Skidmore, Owens, and Merrill, designed this tower. Previously, Skidmore, Owens, and Merrill had gained fame for Chicago's Sears (now Willis)
15 Tower. The title of tallest building was held by that U.S. skyscraper for over 25 years. Now the team has brought international fame to the Middle East with the Burj Khalifa.

The Burj Khalifa

In addition to its record-breaking height, the tower's shape also stands out from other buildings of its time. Approaching Dubai from the desert, the Burj Khalifa appears as a **refined**, classic[1] form rising above the city. The architects designed a **logical** shape, rather than giving the tower unusual curves or balancing its **bulk** on a narrow edge. Instead, to viewers, it looks like the simpler skyscrapers from generations ago.

In fact, the tower is surprisingly subtle[2] for a structure of its size. While its base looks wide, the building **transforms** as it rises. It narrows into a single sharp point at the top. You'd never guess that the tip is made of 4,000 tons of steel and is used to house the building's communications equipment.

If you are looking up at the tower from the ground nearby, you'll notice the nearly 26,000 panes of individually cut glass. The surfaces of aluminum and stainless steel shine in the bright sun, almost year-round. Of course, when standing close to the building, it's impossible to see the top.

The Burj Khalifa's height is experienced best from inside the tower. Once inside, you find more records that the Burj Khalifa has broken. Ride one of its 57 elevators to the top and you will have traveled the longest distance possible in an elevator. Exit the elevator at the observation deck and you will be on the highest outdoor observation area in the world. Look out at the **abstract** beauty of the world from this height. Then take the elevator down two floors.

There you can dine at a slightly more comfortable height.

As impressive as the height is, it's the **dynamic** relationship of the interior to the exterior that gives the building purpose and form. A concrete core supports the weight of the tower and sits in the center of a Y-shaped floor plan. This core and Y-shape provide stability on the ground and in the air, and as the building rises, the floors become narrower, creating a stair-step appearance. **Furthermore**, the curving sections of the Y-shape reduce the effect of the wind. The firm describes this as "confusing the wind." Because of the different widths of the floors, the wind cannot form a **cycle** of force circling around the tower. **Hence**, the narrowing of the tower has a structural purpose too.

This unique design is made possible by the **allocation** of the interior real **estate**. The **bulk** of the building is **comprised** of condominiums.[3] This is key. If the tenants[4] in the building were companies looking for office space, the slim design would not have been possible. Companies now want lots of space for desks and office machinery. However, a building **comprised** mainly of condominiums can be designed without all the requirements for huge, open floors.

Whether you are seeing the Burj Khalifa from far away, nearby, or from the inside, tilt your head back and enjoy the view. Human creativity doesn't get any better than this.

---

[1] *classic:* having a value that will last a long time
[2] *subtle:* not large, bright, or easy to notice
[3] *condominium:* an apartment owned by the people who live in it
[4] *tenant:* a person that pays to use another person's property

LEARN

Descriptive writing uses vivid details to help readers create pictures in their minds. Use these methods to include descriptions in your writing.

1. Adjective-noun combinations such as *large office* and *ancient building* create an image.

2. Some verbs, such as *twist, bend, transform,* and *illuminate,* are descriptive and add to the image.

3. Some verbs, such as *is, seem, become, appear, look,* and *feel,* link a noun with a description.

              linking verb   adjective
   In fact, the tower *is* surprisingly *subtle* for a structure of its size. While its base

  linking verb   descriptive verb
   looks wide, the building *transforms* as it rises.

Other descriptive language gives practical details. Most architecture reviews describe building details or give technical construction information.

You'd never guess that the tip is made of 4,000 tons of steel and is used to house the building's communications equipment.

APPLY

A. Read the architecture review on pages 2–3 again. Find descriptive language in the model.

1. Circle adjective-noun combinations that create an image.

2. Underline descriptive verbs.

3. List three verbs that link an image with a description.

   appears, _____

B. Work with a partner to find examples of descriptive and technical language in the writing model. Write them in the chart below.

Descriptive language (helps to create a picture)	Technical language (used mainly in architecture)
creating a stair-step appearance	*a concrete core supports the weight of the tower*

C. Write more descriptive versions of each sentence. Share your sentences with a partner.

1. The sunset is beautiful.

   The sunset paints the sky with red and orange light.

2. The building is tall.

   _____

3. The space is small.

   _____

4. The food tastes good.

   _____

Analyze

A. Read the architecture review on pages 2–3 again. The author compares the Burj Khalifa to other structures. Answer the questions below.

1. Where are the comparisons in the review? Find and underline the comparisons.

2. What language patterns express comparisons? Write the phrases.

   stands out from _____

   _____

   _____

   _____

   _____

3. How do the comparisons help create a picture of the building? Discuss your opinion with a partner.

B. Find a sentence in the architecture review on pages 2–3 that expresses the same idea as each sentence below.

1. The tower is taller than other skyscrapers.

   At 828 meters tall, it towers over other great skyscrapers.

2. As the building rises, it changes shape.

   _____

3. The building doesn't try to be different.

   _____

C. With a partner, read the pairs of sentences in activity B. Which sentence in each pair is more descriptive? Discuss what makes the author's better.

D. Discuss these questions with a partner.

1. Why does the author compare the Burj Khalifa to the Willis Tower?

2. Why does the author discuss the floor plan of the building?

3. What descriptions from the model best created a picture of the building in your mind?

4. What practical and technical details do you think are the most interesting?

Vocabulary Activities   STEP I: Word Level

A. Match each cycle to its parts. Then compare answers with a partner. What other cycles can you think of?

_c_ 1. life cycle

____ 2. lunar (moon) cycle

____ 3. water cycle

____ 4. wash cycle (for laundry)

a. fill, soak, rinse, wash, spin

b. first quarter, full, last quarter, new

c. birth, childhood, adulthood, death

d. precipitation (rain, snow), evaporation, cloud formation

B. Something that is *abstract* exists as an idea, but you cannot touch or see it. The opposite of *abstract* is *concrete*. You can see and feel concrete things. Write *A* for abstract nouns and *C* for concrete nouns.

_C_ 1. skyscraper

____ 2. research

____ 3. window

____ 4. friendship

____ 5. bicycle

____ 6. university

One definition of *logic* is "a sensible reason or way of thinking." The adjective form, *logical*, describes "something that seems natural or sensible."

*It's **logical** to cancel the game, because it looks like it is going to rain.*

The opposite, *illogical*, means "not sensible or not reasonable."

*Since transportation is expensive, living so far away from school is **illogical**.*

CORPUS

C. Read the decisions below. Write *L* if a decision is logical, and *I* if it is illogical.

_L_ 1. The floor plan included both stairs and an elevator.

____ 2. He designed a building with 85 floors and one elevator.

____ 3. Road construction was performed in the morning, when many people were driving to work.

____ 4. The pilot delayed her flight because of a storm.

A *colleague* is "a person who you work with."

Use the word *colleague* in formal situations, such as in the workplace or at a business lunch.

Colleague usually refers to a person who is at your level. For instance, you would not refer to your manager as a colleague.

*Let me introduce you to my **colleague**. We've worked together for seven years.*

CORPUS

D. Read the word lists below. Circle the synonym for *colleague* in each list.

1. coach	(business associate)	classmate
2. assistant	friend	coworker
3. collaborator	manager	opponent
4. work partner	instructor	employee

E. Complete each sentence below using the correct form of *allocate*, *obtain*, or *refine*. Use the words in parentheses for help.

1. I _____*obtained*_____ my passport only five days before my trip!
   (received)

2. Over the next week, the architect will _____ these blueprints.
   (improve)

3. This apartment has a lot of space _____ to the kitchen.
   (set aside)

4. Do you know where I could _____ a building permit?
   (get)

F. Complete the excerpt from an architecture review with the correct form of a target word from the box. Use the words in parentheses for help. Compare answers with a partner.

| allocate | bulk | futhermore | hence |
| obtain | real estate | refine | transform |

Spanish architect Santiago Calatrava designed the Turning Torso, the

tallest building in Sweden and all of Scandinavia. It looks like a building

waving in the wind, twisting as it rises. _____*Furthermore*_____, its base is
                                           (1. In addition)

smaller than its highest point. _____, its form doesn't seem quite
                                (2. As a result)

logical. Each of Calatrava's buildings seems to be better than the last. He

_____ his reputation from this ability to _____ his
(3. got)   (4. improve)

work. He _____ buildings into sculptures. The _____
         (5. turns)   (6. majority)

of the Turning Torso is comprised of apartments. However, Calatrava

_____ some of the _____ to be used as a spa
  (7. assigned)   (8. space)

and lounge.

Vocabulary Activities STEP II: Sentence Level

Comprise means "to have someone or something as parts or members." In
this sense, something is made up of other things.

> The exhibit **comprises** 14 original artworks.

When using this sense of *comprise*, the collocation *be comprised of* is common:

> The group is **comprised** of men and women from each geographic region.

Comprise can also mean "to be the parts or members that form something."
In this sense, *comprise* means to consist of the things mentioned. Do not use
be comprised of with this sense of *comprise*.

> Young people **comprise** the largest group of social media users.

> ✗ Young people are **comprised** of the largest group of social media users.

CORPUS

G. Create sentences using the phrases below and the verb *comprise*. Use the verb
    comprise in two sentences and the collocation *be comprised of* in two sentences.

1. building / offices and stores

    The building I work in is comprised of offices and stores.

2. architects and engineers / bulk of the design team

    _____

3. apartment building / 400 units

    _____

4. estate / main house and gardens

    _____

H. *Dynamic* describes something that is full of energy or ideas. What makes the
    Burj Khalifa's design dynamic? Use *dynamic* and *transform* in your answer.

    _____

    _____

Grammar | Passive and Active Voice

Active Voice

In the sentence below, the subject is the agent (or doer) of the action. This is called active voice. Use the active voice to focus on the person or thing that does the action.

agent   agent   action   receiver
Adrian Smith and William Baker _designed_ **the tower.**

Passive Voice

In the sentence below, the subject is the receiver of the action. This is called passive voice. The passive voice contains a form of the verb *be* and the past participle of the main verb.

receiver   action   agent   agent
The tower _was designed_ **by Adrian Smith and William Baker.**

Writers use the passive voice when they want to focus on the person or thing that the action happened to. Passive voice is also used when the agent is unknown or unimportant.

receiver   action
The building _was constructed_ **over several years.**

The passive voice can only be used with transitive verbs, which describe actions someone or something can do to another person or thing. Intransitive verbs, such as *appear*, *look*, *occur*, and *emerge*, cannot take the passive voice.

The transitive verbs *has*, *lack*, *weighs*, and *consists of* do not take the passive voice.

A. Read the sentences below. Write *A* for active and *P* for passive voice. Then rewrite the sentence in the other voice with a partner. Discuss why the writer used the active or passive voice in each sentence.

_A_ 1. Its Y-shaped floor plan provides stability.

    Stability is provided by its Y-shaped floor plan.

____ 2. A concrete core supports the weight of the tower.

____ 3. The bulk of the building is comprised of condominiums.

B. Read the focus of each sentence. Is the voice used appropriate for the focus? Write *A* for agree or *D* for disagree. If you disagree, rewrite the sentence appropriately.

_A_ 1. *Focus on what happened*: My computer was finally fixed by a colleague from the technical support staff. _____

____ 2. *Focus on the architect*: The sculpture was designed by the famous architect Zaha Hadid. _____

____ 3. *Focus on the task*: The Taglia engineering firm did the review on these building plans. _____

____ 4. *Focus on the museum*: The Lima Art Museum obtained a new painting by Picasso. _____

____ 5. *Focus on the architecture review*: A magazine published the architecture review of the Burj Khalifa. _____

C. Find sentences in the writing model on pages 2–3 that use the passive voice. What does each sentence focus on?

1. Passive sentence: *The Burj Khalifa's height is experienced best from inside.*

   Sentence focus: *how tall the Burj Khalifa is*

2. Passive sentence: _____

   Sentence focus: _____

3. Passive sentence: _____

   Sentence focus: _____

4. Passive sentence: _____

   Sentence focus: _____

5. Passive sentence: _____

   Sentence focus: _____

WRITING SKILL | Spatial Organization

LEARN

When writing an architecture review, help your readers imagine the building by organizing your writing based on where things are located. Many architecture reviews follow the natural order of stages in which a person would see a building. Here are common ways to do this:

- Bottom to top: Begin your description at the bottom of the building and end at the top.

- Far to near: Describe a building by how it looks from far away, then how it looks when standing closer, and finally how it looks when inside building.

Use phrases that tell where something is located compared to something else. The chart below contains useful words and phrases:

Prepositions: above, below, between, across from, behind, in front of, next to	The Petronas Towers consist of two buildings with a bridge <u>between</u> them.
Directions: left, right, up, down, north, south, east, west	A garden spreads <u>to the left</u> and <u>to the right</u> of the grand entrance.
Adverbs of location: upward, downward, toward	The ceiling curves <u>toward</u> the walls.

APPLY

A. Read the architecture review on pages 2–3. Write sentences you find that use words or phrases indicating location. Circle those words or phrases.

1. *A concrete core sits (in the center) of a Y-shaped floor plan.*

2. _____

3. _____

4. _____

B. Read the writing model again. Identify the order in which the details below appear in the review. What spatial organization does the writer use?

_4_ description of the building's interior structure

____ description of the building's exterior appearance from nearby

____ description of the building's exterior appearance from far away

____ description of the building's interior that people can see

Spatial Organization: _____

Collaborative Writing

A. Which of the following aspects are interesting to you about a building? Write *1* for "very interesting," *2* for "somewhat interesting," and *3* for "not interesting."

____ its age   ____ how popular it is

____ where it's located   ____ what it's used for

____ the name of its architect   ____ what the outside looks like

____ how much it cost to build   ____ what the inside looks like

B. Work in a small group. Discuss the aspects of a building that you agree are interesting. Use the notes below to decide what details to include in an architectural review of the Guangzhou Opera House.

Notes	
Architect	Zaha Hadid
Project	• Guangzhou Opera House • consists of two buildings: 1. opera theater, 2. public auditorium • completed in 2010 • construction cost $200 million
Location	• Guangzhou, China • next to the Pearl River • surrounded by modern skyscrapers
Materials	• steel structure • glass and granite exterior
Comparisons	The walkways that surround the buildings look like the stair-step landscape of vineyards or rice fields.
Interior description	• huge lobbies with no columns • lines of small lights in the staircases and ceilings • wide staircases lead to the theater, which has curving shapes designed to improve the sound of the opera • 4,000 lights hang overhead in the theater
Exterior description	• two buildings with rough, uneven shapes • ramps circle the two buildings • steel frame exterior covered in triangular glass and stone tiles • buildings are on opposite sides of a plaza
Opinion	The building is very unique. It transforms an ordinary business neighborhood into an artistic place.

C. Discuss these questions with your group.

1. Which method of spatial organization is best for a review of this building?

2. What words and phrases of location will help your readers understand your description?

D. Work with your group to write an architectural review of the Guangzhou Opera House. Use the information in the chart.

E. Share your architecture review with the class. As a class, discuss the questions below.

1. What type of spatial organization does the architecture review use?

2. Where are the interior descriptions? Where are the exterior descriptions?

3. Did the details included make the review interesting?

4. Did spatial organization help make the description of the building easier to understand? Why, or why not?

Independent Writing

A. Choose a building that you would like to review. It can be a building that exists or one that you would create. Use the chart to organize details you'd like to include.

	Notes
Architect	
Project	
Location	
Materials	
Comparisons	
Interior description	
Exterior description	
Opinion	

B. Review the comparisons you underlined in the writing model. What can you compare your building or structure to? Write two comparisons below.

It is easily twice as tall as New York's Empire State Building. _____

_____

_____

C. What spatial organization will you use in your review? _____

D. Write an architecture review. Use the information from activities A, B, and C. Include descriptive language and the target words from page 1. Use the active or passive voice to focus on the most important parts of your sentences.

A. Read your architecture review. Answer the questions below, and make revisions to your review as needed.

1. Check (✓) the information you included in your architecture review.

   ☐ name of architect   ☐ names of the materials used

   ☐ name and location of building   ☐ comparisons to other buildings

   ☐ description of the interior   ☐ opinion

   ☐ description of the exterior

2. Look at the information you did not include. Would adding that information make your review more interesting and help readers picture the building?

Grammar for Editing   Paragraph Format

In a piece with more than one paragraph, it's necessary to separate each paragraph. There are two common methods:

1. Block paragraphs: The first line of the paragraph starts at the left margin, like the other lines. Put an extra blank line between paragraphs to separate them.

Block paragraphs are most often used in newspapers, magazines, websites, and business writing.

2. Indented paragraphs: The first line of the paragraph starts several spaces to the right of the other lines, showing where a new paragraph begins. There are no extra lines between paragraphs.

Indented paragraphs are most often used in academic writing.

B. Check the language in your architecture review. Revise and edit as needed.

Language Checklist
☐ I used target words in my architecture review.
☐ I used descriptive and technical language.
☐ I used passive and active voice where appropriate.
☐ I separated my paragraphs visually.

C. Check your architecture review again. Repeat activities A and B.

Self-Assessment Review: Go back to page 1 and reassess your knowledge of the target vocabulary. How has your understanding of the words changed? What words do you feel most comfortable using now?

UNIT 2

Ready to Bike?

In this unit, you will

> analyze a questionnaire and summary of results and learn how they are used in urban planning.

> using classification in writing.

> increase your understanding of the target academic words for this unit.

WRITING SKILLS

> Audience and Purpose

> Writing about Data

> **GRAMMAR** Modals of Certainty

Self-Assessment
Think about how well you know each target word, and check (✓) the appropriate column. I have...

TARGET WORDS	never seen the word before.	heard or seen the word but am not sure what it means.	heard or seen the word and understand what it means.	used the word confidently in *either* speaking or writing.
AWL				
compile				
cooperate				
correspond				
equate				
🔑 factor				
gender				
🔑 grant				
incidence				
🔑 income				
initiate				
🔑 justify				
mode				
offset				
🔑 relevant				

🔑 Oxford 3000™ keywords

Building Knowledge

Read these questions. Discuss your answers in a small group.

1. What do you think is the best way to collect information from a large number of people?

2. Would you prefer to complete a questionnaire online, in writing, or in person?

3. Have you ever completed a questionnaire? What was it about?

Writing Model

Questionnaires and surveys are used to find out about people's opinions or behaviors. A summary presents the results of the questionnaire. Read a summary about a questionnaire conducted to investigate a bike-sharing program.

Budapest Department of Transportation Bike-Sharing Evaluation

This report summarizes the findings[1] from a questionnaire about a new bike-sharing program. The program would allow short-term bike rentals throughout Budapest's city center. The questionnaire
5 was given to residents[2] working in the city center. Funding for the study was provided by a **grant** from the city council. A total of 200 participants **cooperated** in the study. The survey asked the respondents[3] about their travel practices. It also
10 evaluated whether it would be possible to replace existing **modes** of transportation with bikes. The chart on this page **corresponds** to the data **compiled** from question 1 of the questionnaire, which asked how respondents currently travel to work.

Results from the questionnaire **justify initiating** a bike-sharing program. Only 26
15 percent of the people surveyed currently commute[4] by bike. However, over 70 percent of respondents who live within 20 miles of their workplace said they would be likely or very likely to commute by bike. More than 90 percent of respondents do live within 20 miles of their workplace. Based on these findings, of the 200 survey participants, nearly 130 may participate in the program.

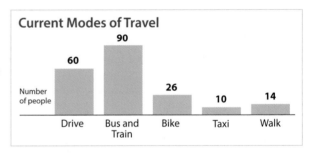

Question 1 responses

---

[1] *finding:* something that is discovered by research
[2] *resident:* a person who lives in a place
[3] *respondent:* a person who answers questions, especially in a survey
[4] *commute:* a trip made regularly from your home to your place of work

20　　Of participants who answered that they leave the office during work hours at least one to three times a month, almost three-quarters said they would be likely or very likely to make those trips by bike. The major reasons for leaving the office were to make short trips, such as running errands[5] or going to lunch. Most of these trips could be made by bike. The major reasons for making the trips by bike were to get exercise, to **offset**

25　pollution, or a combination of both.

　　In conclusion, the program looks likely to increase bike use during business hours. **Income** levels and **gender** were not **factored** into the results, however. Differences based on these **factors** could be **relevant** to the program's outcome.[6] In addition, more research needs to be done on the safety of such a program. The majority of respondents who said

30　they would not use the program **equate** bike riding with injury. They believe that the program may increase the **incidence** of traffic accidents.

---

[5] *run errands:* to make a short trip to get something done, such as buy a few grocery items
[6] *outcome:* the result or effect of something

Questionnaire

1. **Check the modes of transportation that you use most often to commute to work. Check all that apply.**
   - drive
   - public transportation (train and/or bus)
   - bike
   - taxi
   - walk

2. **How far do you live from your place of work?**
   - less than 5 miles
   - 5–10 miles
   - 10–20 miles
   - more than 20 miles

3. **How likely would you be to commute by bike?**
   - ○ not likely (almost never)
   - ○ likely (for at least half of the trips)
   - ○ very likely (for more than half of the trips)

4. **Indicate how often you leave your workplace for the following reasons:**

	Less than once a month	1 to 3 times a month	1 to 3 times a week	Every day
To go to lunch				
To attend meetings				
To exercise				
To run errands				

5. **How likely would you be to make the trips by bike if one were available for you to use during work hours?**
   - ○ not likely (almost never)
   - ○ likely (for at least half of the trips)
   - ○ very likely (for more than half of the trips)

6. **What are the most likely reasons you would participate in the bike-sharing program?**
   - ○ to get places faster
   - ○ to exercise
   - ○ to **offset** pollution caused by cars

7. **What are the most likely reasons you would not participate in the program?**
   - ○ I have safety concerns.
   - ○ I think it's inconvenient.
   - ○ I prefer other **modes** of transportation.

LEARN

Before you write, think about the audience (your readers) and the purpose (the reason you are writing the text). Audience and purpose influence level of formality, what information is included, and how that information is presented.

Analyze two characteristics of your audience:

1. <u>Relationship</u>: What is your connection to your audience? Do you know them as friends, or do you know them from a professional or academic setting?

   This will affect your tone and word choice. Should your tone be friendly or distanced? Is formal language necessary, or can you use casual phrases?

2. <u>Prior Knowledge</u>: What does your audience already know about your topic?

   This will affect the level of detail you include. Will you need to explain any concepts or technical terms? What information does your audience need in order to understand your topic?

Determine your purpose:

1. <u>Persuade</u>: To convince your audience to agree with you, your writing will include your own opinions or a recommendation.

2. <u>Inform</u>: To inform your audience about a topic, your writing will contain facts, but not many opinions.

3. <u>Entertain</u>: To entertain your audience and make them interested in your topic, your writing may tell a story or include humor.

APPLY

A. Read the statements below from the summary and questionnaire on pages 16–18. Match each statement with its purpose.

Statements	Purposes
_c_ 1. Funding for the study was provided by a grant from the city council.	a. state the limitations of the study (what the study didn't do)
___ 2. The survey asked the respondents about their commuting habits. It also evaluated the likelihood of replacing existing modes of transportation with bikes.	b. state the goal of the study
___ 3. Only 26 percent of the people surveyed currently commute by bike. However, over 70 percent of respondents who live within 20 miles of their workplace said they would be likely or very likely to commute by bike.	c. state who paid for the study
___ 4. Income levels and gender were not factored into the results. However, differences based on these factors could be relevant to the program's outcome.	d. summarize a finding

B. Based on the purpose of the statements in activity A, what do you conclude is the overall purpose of the summary? Check (✓) one.

____ to persuade ____ to inform ____ to entertain

C. Read the questionnaire on pages 17–18 again. Which of the following statements about the intended respondents are probably true? Circle all that apply. Discuss your answers with a partner.

a. They are adults.

b. They have children.

c. They know how to drive.

d. They live in or near Budapest.

e. They know how to ride a bike.

Analyze

A. Read the summary on pages 16–17 again. Discuss these questions with a partner.

1. Who would benefit from reading this report?

2. Based on the language in the summary, what type of audience do you think the writer expected?

3. What sentence in the summary states the writer's overall opinion about the bike-sharing program? Why do you think the writer's opinion is located there?

4. What do you think is the writer's main purpose?

B. Read the questionnaire on pages 17–18 again. Discuss these questions with a partner.

1. Question 1 asks participants what mode of transportation they use. Why are researchers collecting this information?

2. Question 2 asks participants how far they live from their workplace, and Question 3 asks how likely participants would be to commute by bike. How are responses to Question 2 and Question 3 related?

3. How does Question 6 help researchers?

4. Why might researchers be interested in Question 7?

5. Why are answers provided for participants to choose from? How does this help both the participants and the researchers?

6. Why doesn't the questionnaire request the participants' names?

C. Look at the graph on page 16. Mark each sentence below as *T* (true) or *F* (false).

_F_ 1. More people walk to work than bike.

____ 2. Fewer than 20 people currently bike to work.

____ 3. The majority of people take public transportation or drive to work.

____ 4. Fourteen percent of people walk to work.

D. Look at the graph on page 16 again. Discuss the questions below with a partner.

1. Why do you think the authors presented this information in a chart?

2. Is there any other information in the summary on pages 16–17 that you think would be easier to understand in a graph or chart?

3. Why would a chart or graph be more helpful to you?

Vocabulary Activities | STEP I: Word Level

A. Add the suffixes *-ion* or *-ation* to change the following verbs into nouns. Use a dictionary to check your new words.

1. compile _compilation_

2. cooperate _____

3. equate _____

4. justify _____

5. initiate _____

B. Complete the paragraph below using the correct form of the target words from activity A. Use the words in parentheses as clues.

To _____*justify*_____ building a new student center, we need to figure out
  (1. give a good reason for)

if student attendance is expected to increase. That would be a reason to build

a new center. We will need _____ from the admissions department
                              (2. participation)

to obtain data on student enrollment in the university. We will need to

_____ the data and make predictions about how many students
  (3. gather)

will be likely to use the student center in the next ten years. After our report

has been reviewed, we hope to _____ discussions with architecture
                                 (4. start)

firms. There are other factors in this _____ besides the number of
                                        (5. final decision)

students attending the university, such as the cost of the project.

Grant has different meanings as different word forms.

1. When *grant* is a noun, it refers to "money that is given by the government or by another organization for a particular purpose."

   *She was awarded a **grant** to continue her research.*

2. *Grant* can also be a verb. One meaning is "to give someone what they ask for, especially formal or legal permission to do something."

   *I was **granted** additional time to stay in the country.*

3. Another meaning is "to agree that something is true, although you may not like or completely agree with it."

   *I **grant** you that he's a nice person, but I wouldn't want to work for him.*

CORPUS

C. Which definition of *grant* is used in each sentence? Write the number of the definition from the corpus box above. Then write your own version of each sentence.

__2__ 1. I was granted permission to take a two-week vacation in March.

   My boss gave me permission to take a two-week vacation in March.

____ 2. The scientist won a research grant to continue her experiments.

   _____

____ 3. He works long hours, I'll grant him that. But he never gets much done.

   _____

____ 4. The bank granted us a loan to start a small business.

   _____

D. Each question below is from a survey about factors that lead to car accidents. Match each survey question with the summary statement it corresponds to. Underline the forms of the target words.

Questions	Summary statements
_b_ 1. How often do you talk on the phone while driving?	a. Using other modes of transportation besides driving offsets the likelihood of car accidents.
____ 2. How many hours a week do you spend driving?	b. The <u>incidence</u> of traffic death is linked to cell-phone use.
____ 3. Check off the modes of transportation you use.	c. More hours spent driving equated with a higher incidence of traffic accidents.
____ 4. How often do you drink coffee while driving?	d. Age corresponded strongly with the rate of accidents.
____ 5. How old are you?	e. Coffee drinking was not as relevant as other factors.

Vocabulary Activities | STEP II: Sentence Level

Incidence refers to "the number of times something (usually bad) happens." It is usually followed by the preposition *of*.

> There is a high <u>**incidence**</u> <u>of</u> neck injuries during automobile accidents.

To describe the rate of *incidence*, use *low* or *high*, not *small* or *big*.

E. Check the nouns that would likely follow *incidences of*. With a partner, discuss the factors that lead to these incidences.

___ employment   ___ heart disease

___ airplane crashes   ___ celebrations

F. Read about the bike-sharing program on pages 16–18 again. Write sentences about how gender, income, and mode of transportation could affect the bike-sharing program's success.

gender: _____

income: _____

mode of transportation: _____

When two things are *equated with* each other, people see them as being equal, or as being the same thing.

> I have always <u>**equated**</u> the beach <u>with</u> relaxation.

Equation is usually used in math to show that two quantities are equal: "3x + 2 = y." However, it can also refer to a complicated or difficult situation.

> When I moved out of my apartment, the high rent was only part of the **equation**.

G. Match each noun in Column I with the quality in Column II that it is often equated with. Then write a sentence about your opinion on each match using a form of the word *equate*.

I	II
_c_ 1. money	a. intelligence
___ 2. good grades	b. travel
___ 3. adventure	c. success

1. _____

2. _____

3. _____

H. Discuss your sentences from activity G with a partner. Do you think it is correct to equate these things with each other? What else do you think can be equated with each of the items in Column I? What else do you think can be equated with each of the items in Column II?

I. Create survey questions to understand someone's views. Use the phrase *equate with* and words from the box for ideas. Then take turns asking and answering the questions with a partner.

beauty	education	family	good health	intelligence
old age	sense of humor	success	wealth	youth

Question 1: _What do you equate with success?_

Answer: _I equate success with happiness._

Question 2: _____

Answer: _____

Question 3: _____

Answer: _____

Question 4: _____

Answer: _____

When something is *relevant*, it is "connected to what you are talking or writing about."

*I brought all the **relevant** documents for my application.*

The antonym is *irrelevant*.

*His advice is **irrelevant** because he has never experienced my situation.*

CORPUS

J. Answer the questions below. Use *relevant* or *irrelevant* in your answer. Explain your responses to a partner.

1. Should a person consider his or her hobbies and interests when choosing a career? Why, or why not?

_____

2. How important is the factor of income to you when you choose a job?

_____

3. Should participants be asked their gender when they complete a survey about biking to work?

_____

4. Is a chart showing the most popular modes of transportation necessary for a summary of a questionnaire on fashion?

_____

Grammar | Modals of Certainty

Use modals of certainty to make predictions and express guesses or inferences. The modal you use shows how certain you are.

If you are <u>absolutely certain</u>, use *will*.

People who get at least seven hours of sleep <u>*will*</u> perform better on tests.

If you are <u>very certain</u>, use *should*.

With more police officers on the road, the incidence of traffic accidents <u>*should*</u> decrease.

If you are <u>somewhat certain</u>, use *may*.

Four-fifths of respondents who said they would not use the program equate bike-riding with injury and think it <u>*may*</u> also increase the incidence of traffic accidents.

If you are <u>less certain</u> about something, use *could* or *might*.

Income levels and gender were not factored into the results, but differences based on these factors <u>*could*</u> be relevant to the program's outcome.

could/might	may	should	will

Less certain   More certain

A. Find the sentences below in the summary on pages 16–17. Complete each sentence with the correct modal. Write *certain, less certain,* or *more certain* to describe the modal you used.

1. Based on these findings, of the 200 survey participants, nearly 130

_____*may*_____ participate in the program. _____*certain*_____

2. Differences based on these factors _____ be relevant to the

program's outcome. _____

3. They believe that the program _____ increase the incidence of

traffic accidents. _____

B. Read the paragraph below.

> In 2006, residents in Drachten, the Netherlands, removed the traffic lights and road signs from their busiest intersection. The intersection was replaced with a roundabout. What happened next led many urban areas around the world to consider doing the same thing. There was a decrease in the incidence of traffic accidents.

C. Imagine that you are going to conduct a study on what residents where you live would think about replacing traffic lights with roundabouts. Write statements that summarize what you expect to find. Use modals of certainty.

1. *They might think that traffic accidents will increase.* _____

2. _____

3. _____

4. _____

D. Read the statements below. How certain are you that these things will happen in cities in the future? Write sentences using a modal of certainty. Discuss your answers with a partner.

1. Flying cars will replace cars on roads.

   I think flying cars could replace cars on roads. _____

2. Homes and stores will be built underground so that more land can be farmed for food.

   _____

3. Computers and robots will do all building and maintenance work.

   _____

4. All large cities will have spaceship launch facilities.

   _____

WRITING SKILL	Writing about Data

LEARN

When summarizing the results of a survey, include examples of the data you collected. There are several ways to write about data:

- Develop a chart or other graphic to show your results. A graphic should focus only on key points. You do not need to include all the data.

- Point out information that was not asked for in the survey, but could be important. Show where more research is needed.

- State the number of participants. A questionnaire that is answered by 500 participants will be more trustworthy than one answered by five.

- Use percentages (75 percent) or fractions (three-fourths) to report findings.

Numbers ending in zero or five are sometimes called round numbers. People can understand round numbers quickly, especially quarters of 100 percent:

25% = *a quarter*   0% = *none*
50% = *half*   100% = *all*
75% = *three-quarters*

50 percent is also associated with the terms *majority*, for "more than half," and *minority*, for "less than half."

> A **majority** of train commuters take the same train every morning.

Some phrases will tell your reader that your data is near a round number:

Less than a round number	More than a round number
We found that **_less than half_** of participants eat breakfast.	We conclude that **_over three-quarters_** of our customers would appreciate a menu change.
Client approval rose by **_almost a quarter_**.	
Nearly all respondents supported the new law.	**_More than a quarter_** of respondents live within an hour of an airport.

APPLY

A. Discuss these questions with a partner.

1. What kinds of texts generally include graphs and charts?

2. Why do texts show a chart and also describe the same information in words?

3. Is it easier for you to understand charts and graphs or written explanations? Why?

B. Read the summary and questionnaire on pages 16–18 again. Underline phrases that indicate a round number.

C. Read the summary on pages 16–17 again. Answer the following questions as a class.

1. Does the writer use percentages or fractions to report findings?

2. What does the writer suggest should be researched further?

Collaborative Writing

A. The findings below are from another study on the bike-sharing program. Add labels to the chart below to summarize the findings. Work together as a class.

> Participants in the bike-sharing questionnaire filled out a follow-up survey. Respondents were divided into three groups based on their income (below $25,000, $25,000–60,000, and above $60,000). The follow-up survey also categorized respondents based on how they commute to work: by driving, on public transportation, by bike, by taxi, or by walking. Out of the 61 people who drove, 4 made below $25,000, 19 made between $25,000–60,000, and 38 made above $60,000. Of the 90 participants that used public transportation, 42 made below $25,000, 40 made between $25,000–60,000, and 8 made over $60,000. Of the 26 people who biked, 2 made below $25,000, 18 made between $25,000–60,000, and 6 made above $60,000. All of the participants who took a taxi made above $60,000. Six of the participants who walked made below $25,000, 2 made between $25,000–60,000, and 14 made above $60,000.

1. Give the chart a title.   2. Label each category.   3. Label each group.

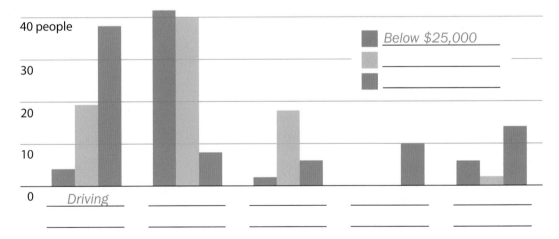

Annual Income and Modes of Travel

B. Does using a chart to present the information above make it easier to understand? Why? Write your answer with a partner.

_____

_____

_____

Independent Writing

A. Pick a project to improve your town. You will write a questionnaire and summary about this project. For example, you might focus on the following topics:

- creating or renovating a park
- improving public transportation
- building a shopping area
- building more homes

Project: _____

B. Define your audience and your purpose. Answer the questions below as a guide.

What do you want to learn from your questionnaire? _____

_____

Who will take your survey? (students, teachers, people in your neighborhood)

_____

Who will read your summary? _____

C. What factors will affect the success of your town improvement project? For example, will people need to visit the park, or shop in local stores? List three factors below.

1. _____

2. _____

3. _____

D. Write a questionnaire of 5–10 questions. Use the factors for success that you wrote in activity C. Include answers for people to choose.

E. Exchange questionnaires with a partner. Take your partner's questionnaire, and provide feedback to help improve it. Revise based on your partner's feedback.

F. Give your questionnaire to classmates or other people who might have opinions on your topic.

G. Summarize your results. Use modals of certainty and the target words from page 15. Include a graph or chart to show part of your data. Explain the purpose of your questionnaire and present your findings. Complete the sentences below as a guide.

1. To explore interest in _____, I created a questionnaire to
   (topic of survey)

   _____.
   (purpose of the questionnaire)

2. A total of _____ participants cooperated in the study.
   (number)

3. Overall, results from the survey show _____.
   (your conclusion based on the survey results)

> **VOCABULARY TIP**
>
> Write survey questions that do not support one opinion.
>
> For example, do not use *Don't you agree* that downtown parking is a problem?
>
> Instead, use a question such as *Do you think* that downtown parking is a problem?

A. Read your questionnaire and summary. Answer the questions below, and make revisions to your summary as needed.

1. Check (✓) the information you included in your summary.

☐ statement of the purpose   ☐ percentages

☐ number of participants   ☐ summary statements

☐ chart or graph   ☐ statement of useful information the survey did not ask for

☐ numbers phrased in a way that's easy to understand   ☐ ideas for follow-up research

2. Look at the information you did not include. Would adding that information make your summary more effective?

Grammar for Editing   Parts of Speech

Use the suffixes *-ation* and *-ion* with nouns. Other common suffixes that appear with nouns are *-ist, -ary,* and *-ory.*

     verb   noun
     compiled → **compilation**

Use the common adjective endings *-ous, -ic, -al, -ian, -able* and *-less.*

     noun   adjective
     cycle → **cyclical**

Many adverbs end in *-ly.*

     adjective   adverb
     regular → **regularly**

B. Check the language in your questionnaire and summary. Revise and edit as needed.

Language Checklist
☐ I used target words in my questionnaire and summary.
☐ I used modals to show certainty.
☐ I used the correct word forms and parts of speech.
☐ I wrote about numbers in a way that is easy to understand.

C. Check your summary and questionnaire again. Repeat activities A and B.

Self-Assessment Review: Go back to page 15 and reassess your knowledge of the target vocabulary. How has your understanding of the words changed? What words do you feel most comfortable using now?

UNIT 3

Alarming Design

In this unit, you will

> analyze product reviews and learn how they are used in art and design.
> use persuasive writing.
> increase your understanding of the target academic words for this unit.

WRITING SKILLS

> Fact and Opinion
> Problems and Solutions
> **GRAMMAR** Adverbial Clauses

Self-Assessment

Think about how well you know each target word, and check (✓) the appropriate column. I have…

TARGET WORDS	never seen the word before.	heard or seen the word but am not sure what it means.	heard or seen the word and understand what it means.	used the word confidently in *either* speaking or writing.
AWL				
🔑 adequate				
attribute				
clause				
🔑 component				
comprehensive				
🔑 criteria				
deduce				
🔑 function				
innovate				
manual				
mechanism				
regulate				
simulate				
straightforward				

🔑 Oxford 3000™ keywords

Building Knowledge

Read these questions. Discuss your answers in a small group.

1. Has a product review ever helped you make a decision about buying a product?

2. Where do you usually find product reviews?

3. What can you learn from a product review?

Writing Model

A product review is usually written by an industry professional to help potential buyers decide if the product is good. Read about three new alarm clocks.

THE WAKE–UP YOU WANT: A REVIEW OF SOME INNOVATIVE ALARM CLOCKS

The problem is no one likes waking up. Solutions abound.[1] Whether it's waking up to music, the soothing sound of the ocean, or sweet-smelling aromas, many companies are trying to make it
5 more pleasant to wake up in the morning. In an effort to narrow down the selection, I evaluated three **innovative** new alarm clocks. The **criteria** I used to evaluate them were price, success at waking me, and design. Although these reviews
10 obviously don't offer a **comprehensive** list of what is available, I have highlighted some of the unique concepts that are being produced.

BROOKSTONE FLOATING MESSAGE ALARM CLOCK

15 The date and time appear to float in the air above this clock. It uses LEDs,[2] which flash rapidly to make the information appear. You can create a personal message along with the date and time. For instance, "Wake up! It's your

20 birthday!" It's important to note, though, that the packaging includes a cautionary **clause**. It warns that the flashing LEDs creating the message display can lead to headaches, nausea, dizziness, and other medical issues. I
25 didn't experience any of these conditions. However, I was distracted by a different **mechanism** on the clock. There's a moving

---

[1] *solutions abound:* there are many available solutions
[2] *LEDs:* light-emitting diodes are devices that produce light

arm that swings back and forth in a soothing[3] way. As I lay there, trying to wake up, I watched the arm swing and it almost put me back to sleep. If it wasn't for the clock's **attribute** of constant beeping, I wouldn't have gotten up that day. Not the effect you want from an alarm clock! But it's worth the $59 because I had such a good time thinking of messages to display. I chose "YOU ARE AWESOME." Who doesn't want to wake up to that?

BIO BRITE EZ WAKE SUNRISE CLOCK

As the name suggests, this clock is supposed to make waking up easy (EZ). Natural light helps our bodies **regulate** sleep, and the clock **simulates** waking up to natural light. The alarm clock glows increasingly brighter for about 30 minutes before your selected wake-up time.

However, after this "natural" approach to waking up, the clock then emits[4] a sound that nobody would describe as natural. The loud beeping destroys all sense of peace and quiet. The clock itself is comprised of simple **components**: a light bulb inside a plastic ball. Along with its simple construction, it is **straightforward** to use. I only had four buttons to choose from. However, at just below $90, I don't think that fewer functions are an advantage. In addition, it's missing a key button—the snooze![5] While the **simulation** of sunrise did help ease me into morning, I don't feel that the clock is worth the high price.

SMASH ALARM CLOCK

The most interesting clock I reviewed was the Smash Alarm. You've probably already **deduced** that you silence this alarm by hitting it instead of by pushing a button. Because of this feature, the Smash Alarm appeals to those of us who really don't enjoy getting up in the morning. If you are one of those people who has to set more than one alarm, or if finding buttons **manually** is too much for you in the early hours of the morning, you may enjoy hitting your alarm.

This small, round alarm is simply designed. It's soft, so you can see the shape of your hand on it after you hit it, which I found to be very satisfying.[6] It certainly made me feel better about getting out of bed! Because this alarm does an **adequate** job of waking even very deep sleepers, I feel that it's a good purchase at $40. For an extra $5, you can buy a two-year warranty. Since you'll be hitting the alarm every morning, I think you might need that warranty!

---

[3] *soothing:* makes someone feel calm and less unhappy
[4] *emit:* to send out something such as a smell, a sound, smoke, heat, or light
[5] *snooze:* to sleep. The "snooze button" on an alarm clock lets a person sleep for a few minutes before the alarm goes off again.
[6] *satisfying:* makes someone feel pleased or happy

LEARN

When writing a product review, your purpose is to inform the reader and give your opinion. Readers need to learn about the product, and they use your opinion to help them form their own opinions.

The *facts* in your review are basic details that can be proven, and that are the same for everyone who uses the product.

The *opinions* in your review are details of your own experience with the product. You can use phrases such as *I think...*, *I feel...*, or adjectives to indicate that a statement is an opinion.

For any opinion, the opposite opinion is also valid. A fact is true for every person, and there is no valid argument against it.

Statement	Could this be true for one person, but not true for someone else?	Fact or opinion?
Size is the most important aspect of a hotel room.	Yes. Room size might be important to one person but less important to someone else.	Opinion
The largest room costs ¥4,000 per night.	No. Room prices are the same for every person.	Fact

APPLY

A. Read the statements below. If the information is a fact, write *F*. If the information is an opinion, write *O*. Compare your answers with a partner.

Floating Message Alarm Clock

_F_ 1. It uses LEDs, which flash rapidly to make the information appear.

____ 2. The packaging includes a cautionary clause.

____ 3. But it's worth the $59 because I had such a good time thinking of messages to display.

____ 4. You can create a personal message along with the date and time.

EZ Wake Sunrise Clock

____ 5. Natural light helps our bodies regulate sleep, and the clock simulates waking up to natural light.

____ 6. The alarm clock glows increasingly brighter for about 30 minutes before your selected wake-up time.

____ 7. The loud beeping destroys all sense of peace and quiet.

____ 8. At just below $90, I don't think that fewer functions are an advantage.

Smash Alarm Clock

___ 9. The most interesting clock I reviewed was the Smash Alarm.

___ 10. This small, round alarm is simply designed.

___ 11. Because this alarm does an adequate job of waking even very deep sleepers, I feel that it's a good purchase at $45.

___ 12. For an extra $5, you can buy a two-year warranty.

B. In a review, facts and opinions often appear in the same paragraph. Read the review below. Underline the facts and circle the opinions.

At $35, the Daylong Messenger Bag is (the best option) if you want to buy an everyday bag without spending a lot of money. Its main pocket is 15 inches tall and 18 inches wide, which is big enough to fit several notebooks, a small laptop or tablet computer, and a lunch container. Other large bags I've owned have been uncomfortable when they held all of my supplies for the day. The Daylong Messenger Bag has soft padding where the bag rests on your shoulder, though, which made all that weight easier to carry. I received another pleasant surprise while using this bag. It is waterproof, so even in the rain, your papers and electronics will stay dry. With two zippered pockets on the outside for my phone and wallet, this is almost the perfect bag. I wish that the large inside pocket was divided into two, though, so that I could separate my lunch from my other supplies. In addition, I noticed that some of the stitches at the corners of the bag were coming loose after only a week. That is easy to repair, but it made me worry about the bag's overall sturdiness.

C. Put a check (✓) next to the words or phrases in activity B that helped you identify opinions. Discuss your answers with a partner.

Analyze

A. Read the alarm clock reviews on pages 32–33 again. Then discuss the questions below with a partner.

1. What facts about alarm clocks do readers need?

2. Whose opinion would you trust for a product review?

3. Does the type of product change whose opinion you trust?

4. Where does the writer's recommendation appear in the reviews? How would the reviews be different if the recommendation came first?

5. Is there other information you want to know about each alarm clock?

B. Read the three product reviews again and complete the chart below with a partner. What information is included in all three reviews?

Type of information	Floating Message Alarm Clock	EZ Wake Sunrise Clock	Smash Alarm Clock
Description of what the alarm can do	✓		
Description of the alarm's design and what it is made of			
Price			
Description of how the alarm sounds			
Who the writer feels the alarm is best for			
Writer's opinion and overall recommendation			

C. Answer the questions below. Discuss your answers in a small group.

1. A review describes what makes a product different from other, similar products. What makes each alarm clock unique? Write your answers below.

    Floating Message Alarm Clock: _It floats a customized message._

    EZ Wake Sunrise Clock: _____

    Smash Alarm Clock: _____

2. Underline the statement in each review that you think best argues for or against the product.

3. Did the writer's opinion influence your own feelings about the products? How?

A. The target words listed below are in the word forms that appear in the writing model. Use a dictionary to list the additional word forms.

Word Form Chart			
Noun	**Verb**	**Adjective**	**Adverb**
function	function	*functional*	*functionally*
		innovative	_____
	regulate		_____
	simulate		_____
	_____	adequate	
_____	_____	straightforward	_____
attribute		_____	_____
	deduce	_____	_____
_____	_____	comprehensive	
	_____		manually

B. Complete the review of Clocky, an alarm clock that you have to chase. Use the correct word form from activity A. Change verb tense if necessary.

In a market where _____*innovation*_____ is common, Clocky, the alarm
(1. new ideas or inventions)

clock on wheels, stands out. From its name, you may not _____
(2. guess)

that Clocky is designed to jump and roll away from you, but who would think

of that? Although it sounds complex, the idea is actually _____.
(3. simple)

When the alarm sounds, the clock rolls off the nightstand, and you have

to catch it. The company used _____ to test it, and they chose
(4. mimicking reality)

a high speed that _____ well. It was the first alarm clock to get
(5. works)

my teenage son out of bed. I _____ its success to the fact that
(6. connect)

he actually had to chase it. I also tried Clocky and thought it required an

_____ chase. I wish there was a way to _____ its sound,
(7. acceptable)   (8. control)

though. The alarm is extremely loud.

A *criterion* is "the standard that you use when you decide something or form an opinion." The plural form, *criteria*, is more common because when you make a decision, you usually base it on more than one *criterion*.

*What **criteria** will we use to determine who gets the design award?*

CORPUS

C. For each of the criteria below, add an additional criterion to make the list more comprehensive. Then compare answers with a partner.

1. To rate a hotel room: view from the room, quietness, cleanliness, *free Wi-Fi*

2. To determine if a student is learning target vocabulary: can pronounce the word, knows the part of speech, _____

3. To decide what phone to buy: what reviewers have said, size, _____

D. Put a *1* next to items that usually come with an user's manual. Put a *2* next to things you can use for manual work.

__1__ 1. a microwave   ___ 2. a computer   ___ 3. a hammer

___ 4. a shovel   ___ 5. a wrench   ___ 6. a refrigerator

Vocabulary Activities   STEP II: Sentence Level

Attribute has the same form as a noun and as a verb. As a noun, *attribute* means "a quality or feature of someone or something."

*She has many positive **attributes**. Being a hard worker is just one of them.*

As a verb, *attribute* means "to believe that something was caused or done by something or someone." Use the preposition *to* with the verb form.

*He **attributed** his work ethic **to** his dad, who had always worked hard.*

CORPUS

E. Read the sentences. Write *N* if the word *attribute* is a noun and *V* if it's a verb. Then answer the questions using the word *attribute*.

__N__ 1. What do you consider your strongest attribute?

My strongest attribute is my sense of humor.

___ 2. What do you attribute global warming to?

_____

___ 3. What do you think are your city's best attributes?

_____

___ 4. What attributes do you look for in a friend?

_____

F. Use the words in parentheses to answer the questions about the alarm clocks reviewed on pages 32–33.

1. What criteria does the writer use to evaluate the alarm clocks? (comprehensive)

   They aren't comprehensive but include price, design, and success at waking him.

2. How does the EZ Wake Sunrise Clock work? (mechanism)

   _____

3. What does the Smash Alarm Clock look like? (components)

   _____

4. Why does the Floating Message Alarm Clock come with a warning? (clause)

   _____

Function has the same form as a noun and as a verb. As a noun, *function* means "the purpose or work of a person or thing."

The **function** of the snooze button is to let you sleep a little more.

As a verb, *function* means "to work properly, as a thing was designed to do."

After we followed the instructions in the user's manual, the stove **functioned** well.

CORPUS

G. Match each device below with its function. Then write an example of what the device can do. Use a form of the word *function*.

_b_ 1. food blender
____ 2. scanner
____ 3. mobile phone
____ 4. air conditioner

a. To let you call people from any place
b. To turn foods into liquids
c. To make air colder
d. To turn paper images or pages into computer files

1. *A properly functioning food blender can turn tomatoes into tomato sauce.*

2. _____

3. _____

4. _____

Grammar Adverbial Clauses

Like adverbs, adverbial clauses describe or explain verbs. In a sentence with two clauses, the adverbial clause refers to the verb in the main clause. Adverbial clause markers are words that appear at the beginning of the adverbial clause.

To show time, use *when, while, as, before, after, whenever,* or *as soon as*:

           adverbial clause   verb
    As I lay there waiting to feel more awake, I watched the arm swing.

To show a contrast or concession, use *even though, though, although,* or *while*. A contrast shows how two things are different. A concession is used in persuasive writing to say "That's true, but…"

           adverbial clause   verb
    Although this is not a comprehensive list, it highlights some of the most unique products.

To give reasons, use *because, since,* or *due to the fact that*. To show a purpose, use *so that, to,* or *in order to*. You can eliminate the subject after *in order to* or *to*.

                      adverbial clause
    The clock gradually gets brighter *in order to simulate sunrise.*

Use a comma between clauses when the adverbial clause is at the beginning of the sentence.

A. Read the sentences about a new car. Underline the adverbial clauses. Write whether the clause is showing *T* (time), *P* (purpose), *C* (contrast or concession), or *R* (giving a reason).

  _C_ 1. <u>Although Subaru usually makes large sports utility vehicles</u>, the new Subaru BRZ is a small sports car.

_____ 2. While the car hasn't been sold overseas yet, the company is projecting huge sales once it hits the global market.

_____ 3. Because I want to buy a new sports car, I test drove the Subaru BRZ.

_____ 4. As soon as I got on the road, I knew it was the car for me.

_____ 5. I had to race back in order to return the car in time.

B. Read the comments about a rocking chair. First, put brackets around each adverbial clause. Then correct one error in each comment. Errors may be in clause structure, comma use, or an incorrect adverbial clause marker.

1. [Although the color of the chair was supposed to be off–white], it looks more tan.

2. I love the chair! As soon I sat down in it, I was almost asleep.

3. The chair is adequate at best. Even it got good reviews, I find it uncomfortable.

4. The mechanism for the rocking is too loud. In to order make it quieter, I recommend placing it on a rug.

5. It took four weeks for the chair to be delivered. Before it arrived I saw one at a store nearby that would have been better.

WRITING SKILL   Problems and Solutions

LEARN

Reviewers evaluate products by writing about problems and solutions. Items are designed to solve specific problems, and a review states whether the item succeeded.

Consider these questions when writing a review:

- What problem is the product designed to solve?
- What attributes of the product helped it solve that problem?
- Was the product unsuccessful in any way? Did it fail to solve the problem?
- Did the product cause any new problems?

APPLY

A. Read the writing model on pages 32–33 again. Match each problem below with the alarm clock that was designed to solve it.

a. Floating Message Alarm Clock

b. EZ Wake Sunrise Clock

c. Smash Alarm Clock

__c__ It can be difficult to locate buttons in the early morning.

____ Different people like to wake up to different messages.

____ The snooze button sometimes allows people to stay in bed too long.

____ Some people feel annoyed when their alarm wakes them up.

____ Many people need to wake up before the sun has risen.

B. Read the alarm clock review below. Underline the phrases that describe problems and circle the phrases that describe solutions.

(Having the radio wake me up,) instead of <u>angry-sounding beeps</u>, was a major advantage of the AlarmBand clock. Listening to music made me feel happier to be starting my day. The next morning, though, I was so interested in the news that I stayed in bed listening for an extra ten minutes! I have to keep the radio set to a music station. Finally, the AlarmBand has no battery, so it turns off if it becomes unplugged. It was stressful making sure the clock always stayed connected to electricity.

C. Read the AlarmBand review on page 41 again. Discuss the questions below with a partner.

1. Which problem or problems was the product designed to solve?

2. Which problem or problems were actually created by the product?

3. Which problems had solutions? Which did not?

Collaborative Writing

A. Read the review of the bag on page 35 again. Answer the questions below with a partner.

1. What problems does the reviewer find with the bag?

2. Which problem is due to the product's design?

3. Which problem is due to the product's quality?

B. Think about bags or backpacks you have used. With your partner, make a list of three problems that can occur when using a bag or backpack.

1. _____

2. _____

3. _____

C. With your partner, rewrite the part of the review on page 35 that discusses problems with the product. Use issues from the list you created in activity B. Complete the sentences below as a guide. You may write about a bag or a backpack.

Unfortunately, the bag/backpack _____.

While the bag/backpack impressed me in many ways, _____

_____

After finding so much to like about the bag/backpack, I was disappointed

when _____

_____, which I did not expect.

D. Share your rewritten portion of the review with the class. As a class, discuss these questions.

1. Have you ever experienced the problems described in the review?

2. Can you think of solutions to the problems mentioned in the review?

3. Does reading about these problems make you more or less likely to buy the bag or backpack?

Independent Writing

A. Choose a product to review. Think about a recent purchase you made, something you want to buy, or something that you find useful.

B. What problem is the product designed to solve? For example, does it make a difficult task easier? Does it make an experience more pleasant? Does it help to save money or time? Is it an improved version of other, similar products?

Problem: _____

Product's solution: _____

C. Fill in the chart with your criteria for evaluation. Use the questions below as a guide.

1. What attributes, or criteria, will help you decide whether or not to recommend the product?

2. What facts about the product's design are related to each criterion?

3. In your opinion, does the product successfully meet each criterion?

Criterion #1:	Fact: Opinion:
Criterion #2:	Fact: Opinion:
Criterion #3:	Fact: Opinion:
Overall recommendation:	

D. Read the sentences below from the clock reviews on page 32–33. Then describe your own experience using the product you are reviewing.

As I lay there, trying to wake up, I watched the arm swing and it almost put me back to sleep.

_____

E. Write a product review. Use the chart from activity C to plan your writing. In your writing, use target words from page 31 and phrases from activities B and D.

> **VOCABULARY TIP**
>
> Describe your experience with the product to make a review interesting. Use phrases such as *when I...*, *after I...*, and *even though I...* to tell your story about using the product.

A. Read your review. Answer the questions below, and make revisions to your review as needed.

1. Check (✓) the information you included in your product review.

   ☐ name of the product

   ☐ criteria for recommendation

   ☐ problems and solutions

   ☐ facts and opinions about the product

   ☐ overall recommendation

   ☐ your experience with the product

2. Look at the information you did not include. Would adding that information make your review more helpful or persuasive to readers?

Grammar for Editing | Fragments and Run-on Sentences

Remember that every sentence needs to have at least one independent clause, which includes a subject and a verb.

     dependent clause   independent clause

While I didn't experience any of these conditions, I was dazed by the alarm clock.

An adverbial clause without an independent clause is a fragment.

    ✗ While I didn't experience any of these conditions.

Sentences that contain more than one independent clause without a conjunction are run-on sentences. To fix a run-on sentence, break the sentence into two sentences or punctuate with a comma and a conjunction (*and, or, but,* or *so*).

    ✗ I evaluated three alarm clocks my criteria were price, volume, and design.

    I evaluated three alarm clocks, and my criteria were price, volume, and design.

B. Check the language in your product review. Revise and edit as needed.

Language Checklist
☐ I used target words in my product review.
☐ I used adverbial clauses to show time, purpose, reason, or concession or contrast.
☐ I corrected any sentence fragments and run-on sentences.
☐ I used adjectives to express my opinions.

C. Check your product review again. Repeat activities A and B.

Self-Assessment Review: Go back to page 31 and reassess your knowledge of the target vocabulary. How has your understanding of the words changed? What words do you feel most comfortable using now?

UNIT 4

Awareness Is Prevention

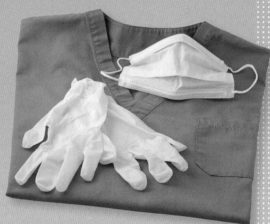

In this unit, you will

> analyze an informational brochure and learn how it is used in public health awareness.
> use an extended definition.
> increase your understanding of the target academic words for this unit.

WRITING SKILLS

> Organizing Information
> Extended Definition
> **GRAMMAR** Adjective Clauses

Self-Assessment

Think about how well you know each target word, and check (✓) the appropriate column. I have…

TARGET WORDS	never seen the word before.	heard or seen the word but am not sure what it means.	heard or seen the word and understand what it means.	used the word confidently in *either* speaking or writing.
AWL				
🔑 acquire				
🔑 aid				
🔑 appropriate				
🔑 assume				
🔑 contract				
🔑 finance				
🔑 instance				
intervene				
isolate				
mediate				
🔑 period				
🔑 reverse				
voluntary				
widespread				

🔑 Oxford 3000™ keywords

Building Knowledge

Read these questions. Discuss your answers in a small group.

1. Think about something you do to prevent yourself from getting sick. How did you learn this habit?

2. If you have a question about health, how do you usually find the answer?

3. What do you think is the best way to teach the public about health issues?

Writing Model

Informational brochures on health issues are often available at health care facilities and online. They make people aware of health issues and improve their health practices. Read this informational brochure about the bacteria MRSA.

Superbug Is a Super Threat

WHAT IS MRSA?

For years, medical researchers have been trying to **reverse** the effects of *superbugs*. What are superbugs? They are a type of bacteria[1] that antibiotics cannot kill. Antibiotics are used to treat[2] bacterial infections, which include everything from common earaches to more serious illnesses. Because of this
5 overuse, some bacteria have become resistant[3] and no longer respond to antibiotics. This has caused **widespread** outbreaks of infections, some of which have become deadly.

Health care professionals classify any bacteria that multiple drugs cannot kill as *multi-drug resistant organisms*, also known as superbugs. The
10 antibiotic-resistant bacteria *Staphylococcus aurus* (MRSA) is one of those superbugs. It is a form of a bacteria called staph, which used to be treated with the antibiotic methicillin. However, the bacteria have changed so that the medication no longer affects them. Without a way to **intervene**, MRSA infections can lead to life-threatening illnesses.

---

[1] *bacteria:* living things that are too small to be seen with the eye
[2] *treat:* to use medicine or medical care to try to make a sick person well again
[3] *resistant:* not harmed by something

HOW DOES MRSA SPREAD?

Gloves can help prevent the spread of MRSA.

15   People usually associate MRSA with hospitals because it is easy for the bacteria to spread from person to person in that environment. The germs are spread by skin-to-skin contact. This means that the germ can be passed on simply by touching an infected person. Once the germ is on a person's skin, it is more likely to enter the body. Unfortunately, this can occur in **instances**
20 of surgery or other medical procedures, when MRSA enters the body through open wounds. In hospitals, it often only takes a brief **period** of time for many people to **acquire** MRSA.

Many people in the hospital are also fighting other illnesses, which has weakened their immune systems, the body's natural defense against disease.
25 It is difficult for this system to fight off additional bacteria when it is already fighting an infection. This makes a person more likely to **contract** MRSA.

However, cases are not **isolated** to hospitals. They also occur in
- other health care facilities
- schools and day-care centers
30 • nursing homes
- universities

In addition, food service workers are at risk[4] of spreading the bacteria. If a worker gets MRSA from handling dirty dishes or food from an infected person, then he or she may pass it on by handling food for other people.

WHAT ARE THE SYMPTOMS?

35   One in four people carry the staph bacteria, which live on the skin. In most **instances**, people who carry the bacteria do not become infected. But some do. Red, painful, and swollen skin are common signs of an ordinary staph infection.

---

[4] *at risk:* in danger

MRSA cases, caused by staph bacteria that are resistant to antibiotics, are
40 often more dangerous. Symptoms of MRSA include
- chest pain
- cough or difficulty breathing
- fatigue[5]
- headache
45 - fever and chills
- skin rash

WHAT CAN YOU DO?

Hospitals have health and safety regulations. And businesses are
financing research into finding new antibiotics that can fight the bacteria.
You can help reduce the number of cases, too, by taking **appropriate**
50 **measures**[6] and **assuming** responsibility for your cleanliness:
1. The number one thing you can do to **aid** the effort is to wash your
   hands often.
2. If you are a health care or food service worker, wear gloves while
   you work.
55 3. Practice other good hygiene. Wear clean clothes to your workplace and
   wash your hands after handling dishes or food.
4. Monitor the cleanliness practices of those around you. While most
   people will **voluntarily** submit to this common-sense advice, ask a
   manager to **mediate** any issues that you observe. As a team, review
60 health and safety guidelines and make sure everyone is committed
   to following them.
5. If you think you have any of the symptoms, let your health care
   provider know.

Research shows that these measures can help prevent the spread of
65 superbugs like MRSA. ■

---

[5] *fatigue:* being extremely tired
[6] *measure:* an action that is done for a specific reason

LEARN

Informational pamphlets include basic information and instructions for action. Organize your text to focus readers' attention on key words and ideas.

Subheadings allow readers to quickly locate helpful information. In informational pamphlets, subheadings are often in the form of questions that people may have.

Mosquito Protection for Families ← Heading

Why are mosquitos dangerous? ← Subheading

Insects that bite humans – such as mosquitos – can carry illnesses such as malaria and the West Nile virus.

How can I prevent mosquito bites? ← Subheading

First, remove standing water from your family's environment.

A numbered or bulleted list highlights important information and is easy to read quickly. Use numbering when the order of steps is important.

If you think you have been infected, follow these steps:

1. Visit your health care professional.

2. Use medication to control symptoms such as fever and rash.

3. See your health care professional again a few weeks later to monitor the infection.

Use bullet points when presenting a general list.

First, remove standing water from your family's environment:

· Empty out containers that hold water, such as the bases of plant holders.

· Cover water tank openings with mosquito mesh.

· Drill holes in the bottoms of outdoor garbage containers.

APPLY

A. Organize the following information into a heading, subheading, and bullet points. Discuss your answers with a partner.

Store hot foods at 60° C or higher.   ~~Separate raw and cooked foods.~~
Preventing Listeria Infections   How can I keep my food safe?
Keep meat, milk, and eggs in the refrigerator.

Heading: _____

Subheading: _____

· *Separate raw and cooked foods.* _____

· _____

· _____

B. Read the brochure on pages 46–48 again. Look at how the information is organized. Then answer the questions below.

1. What are the subheadings? Write them here in the order that they appear in the pamphlet.

   What is MRSA?

   _____

   _____

   _____

2. Circle the bulleted lists.

3. Put a check (✓) next to the numbered list.

C. What is the image in the brochure? How does it connect to the brochure's message? Discuss your answers with a partner.

Analyze

A. Read the brochure on pages 46–48 again. The subheadings indicate the main idea of each section. What section of the brochure would each sentence below fit in best? Write the number of the correct subheading next to each sentence.

1. What is MRSA?   2. How does MRSA spread?

3. What are the symptoms?   4. What can you do?

   _3_ Infected skin may also become very dry.

   ____ It is not the only superbug, but it is one of the most common.

   ____ Tell your doctor if you've ever had a staph infection before.

   ____ In fact, preventing MRSA infections is easier than treating them.

   ____ These warning signs could indicate a case of MRSA.

   ____ Health care workers have contact with many patients every day.

B. Look at the bulleted and numbered lists in the brochure on pages 46–48. Discuss these questions with a partner.

1. There are two bulleted lists in the model. What information is listed?

2. As a reader, is seeing this information in bulleted lists different from seeing it in sentences? How?

3. Why do you think the information under the subheading "What can you do?" occurs in a numbered list?

4. Which item is the most important in the numbered list? Where does it appear?

5. What is the brochure's purpose? How does the way the information is organized help with this purpose?

C. Review Unit 2, where you analyzed audience. Discuss these questions with your class.

1. Who do you think is the intended audience for this brochure?

2. How did the intended audience affect the way the writer organized information?

Vocabulary Activities STEP I: Word Level

A. Write the correct target word from the brochure on pages 46–48 in front of or after each word or phrase below. Then complete the passage with the phrases.

_____ the effects   _____ submit to

_____ measures   in most _____

_____ responsibility   _widespread_ outbreak

_____ of time

To reduce the (1) _widespread outbreak_ of the flu this season, please

follow the Health Department's safety regulations. First, we hope that

everyone will (2) _____ a vaccination to prevent contracting the

flu. While it is not possible to (3) _____ of the virus, we can

reduce the number of cases. Every person must begin (4) _____

for his or her own health. Resting and drinking fluids may not make the

(5) _____ you are sick shorter, but it can make the symptoms less

severe. In addition, take (6) _____ to keep others safe. Wash your

hands often, and cover a cough or sneeze. (7) _____ these methods

help prevent the spread of the virus.

B. Fill in the missing word forms and part of speech subheadings in the chart below. Check your answers in a dictionary.

Word Form Chart			
	Verb	**Adjective**	
finance(s)	finance		financially
assumption	_____	_____	
isolation	isolate		_____
	intervene	intervening	_____
	mediate	_____	_____

C. Each word in the box collocates with the word *aid*. With a partner, match each type of aid with the situation below in which it would be needed.

emergency	financial	first	hearing
international	memory	visual	

<u>   financial aid   </u>   an entrepreneur needs money to start a business

_____   students must learn vocabulary words for a test

_____   a man cups his ears when people speak

_____   a child fell and has a small cut

_____   a country could not grow enough food for its citizens

_____   people have been injured in a car accident

_____   a woman cannot read small print

Vocabulary Activities STEP II: Sentence Level

When something is *appropriate*, it is "suitable or right for a situation." *Appropriate* is often followed by the preposition *for*. The noun after *for* tells who or what something is *appropriate for*.

> It's **appropriate** <u>for adults</u> to help children wash their hands.

Appropriate is sometimes followed by an infinitive (*to* + base verb). The infinitive shows what action is the right thing to do.

> It seems **appropriate** <u>to ask</u> anyone visiting the hospital for proper identification.

CORPUS

D. Imagine a friend is asking for advice. Write responses using *appropriate* or *inappropriate* followed by *for* or an infinitive. Explain your advice to a partner.

1. I had a job interview last week, and they haven't called to let me know if I got the job. Do you think I should call them?

   I think it's inappropriate to call them so soon. You should wait another week.
   _____

2. I said something in class that I think may have hurt another student's feelings. Should I apologize or not?

   _____

3. A woman stepped in front of me in a line yesterday. I was angry, but I didn't say anything. Should I have told her that I was in line first?

   _____

4. I think I might have the flu, but I'm not sure. Should I go to work?

   _____

The verbs *acquire* and *contract* are both used to mean "getting a disease."

However, these words aren't exact synonyms. They collocate with different words.

A person can *acquire* skills, knowledge, or a new house, but cannot *contract* them. To *acquire* means "to get or buy something."

> We **acquired** the property a few months after moving to Mumbai.
> X We **contracted** the property a few months after moving to Mumbai.

As a noun, a *contract* is "a written agreement."

> I have a **contract** with a gardener to take care of my yard.

CORPUS

E. Write pairs of sentences below. Use *acquire* or *contract* and one or two words from the box in each pair of sentences. Compare your sentences in small groups.

aid	appropriate	assume	finance	instance
intervene	isolated	mediate	period	reverse

1. *MRSA cases are not isolated to hospitals. In some instances, people acquire the disease in restaurants.*

2. _____

_____

3. _____

_____

4. _____

_____

5. _____

_____

F. You *intervene in* situations but *intervene between* people. In a small group, discuss whether you would intervene in the situations below. Use *intervene in* or *intervene between* in your responses.

1. Riding the train one morning, you overhear two men having an argument.

   I would be too frightened to intervene between two people who were arguing.

2. You see a very young child wandering around a grocery store. It looks like she may be lost.

   _____

3. While waiting for the bus, a person approaches you who needs first aid. He has a cut on his cheek and his arm looks injured.

   _____

4. A shop owner and a customer are talking about the price of an item. You know that the item is not worth the amount of money that the shop owner is asking for.

   _____

For instance is an idiom. It means "for example."

   The Northwest Hospital is very good. <u>For **instance**</u>, it has excellent surgeons.

In most instances is another common phrase. Use this phrase to discuss situations that occur often.

   <u>In most **instances**</u>, people who carry the bacteria don't become infected.

CORPUS

G. Read each statement below. Then write an example for each statement, using the phrase *for instance* or *in most instances*. Compare your sentences with a partner.

1. MRSA can lead to very serious consequences.

   For instance, it can result in death.

2. There are several things you can do to keep it from spreading.

   _____

3. MRSA is not just isolated to hospitals.

   _____

4. Look for signs that someone is infected.

   _____

5. Some illnesses do not respond to antibiotics.

   _____

Grammar | Adjective Clauses

Like adjectives, adjective clauses define or identify nouns. In a sentence with two clauses, the adjective clause can describe any noun in the independent clause.

Begin an adjective clause with the relative pronouns *who* or *that* to refer to people and *which* or *that* to refer to things.

noun   adjective clause
Food service workers *who handle dirty plates* should wash their hands often.

noun   adjective clause
One in four people carry the staph bacteria, *which live on the skin*.

An adjective clause can be used to combine two sentences that have the same topic.

MRSA is resistant to antibiotics.   **Researchers are trying to develop treatments for MRSA.**

noun   adjective clause
Researchers are trying to develop treatments for MRSA, *which is resistant to antibiotics*.

A. Read the paragraph. Place brackets ([ ]) around the adjective clauses. Then circle the noun that each adjective clause is describing.

Your body turns the (food) [that you eat] into glucose. A chemical called

insulin helps your body's cells get the glucose, which they use for energy.

If you have diabetes, the glucose stays in your blood, and your cells don't

get the energy that they need. There are two types of diabetes. In Type 1

diabetes, which usually occurs in childhood, the body does not make insulin.

Type 2 diabetes, which is more common, can occur at any age. In Type 2

diabetes, the body makes insulin but cannot use it correctly.

B. Combine the sentences into one sentence with an adjective clause.

1. You should avoid eating sweets and desserts. These foods are high in sugar.

   You should avoid eating sweets and desserts that are high in sugar.

2. Insulin regulates glucose. Your body needs glucose for energy.

   _____

3. Diabetes is a disease. The disease causes sugar to build up in your blood.

   _____

4. Studies show some people are more at risk of having heart attacks. These people have diabetes.

   _____

WRITING SKILL   Extended Definition

LEARN

Informational brochures are often an extended definition. An extended definition provides a thorough understanding of a single term.

This can include any aspect of the term:

- dictionary definition
- different meanings to different audiences
- related examples or statistics
- historical background
- where or when it is used
- definitions of related terms

When writing an extended definition, decide what aspects of a term are important to your audience. In a health brochure, focus on the information that will affect the public's health.

APPLY

A. Put a check (✓) next to the information that you think would be useful in an extended definition of a public health issue. Discuss your answers with a partner.

☐ Malaria is more dangerous for children than for adults.

☐ Sir Ronald Ross received the 1902 Nobel Prize in Medicine for his malaria research.

☐ Malaria parasites have specific genetic codes shared only by algae.

☐ Sleeping under a mosquito net is a good defense against malaria.

☐ The tourism industry is often harmed in areas where malaria is common.

☐ Doctors treat minor cases of malaria with pills.

☐ Symptoms of malaria include chills and fever appearing every 2–4 days.

B. Choose one of the statements that you did not mark with a check (✓) in activity A. Why shouldn't that information appear in a public health brochure? Write your reason below. Discuss your answer with a partner who wrote about a different statement.

_____

_____

Collaborative Writing

A. Work in a small group. Read the list below and check (✓) the questions you think should be answered in a public health brochure. Add other questions.

☐ How has it been treated in the past?

☐ Who typically contracts or develops it?

☐ What institutions are researching it?

☐ How do doctors treat it?

☐ Is it more common in certain places or regions?

☐ When was the issue first recognized?

☐ How can people learn more about it?

☐ Can it be spread?

☐ Why has this issue become a problem?

☐ Are there ways to prevent it?

☐ What are the symptoms or ways to diagnose it?

☐ Other: _____

☐ Other: _____

☐ Other: _____

B. Look at the chart below. Which details are important to include in an extended definition about diabetes? Decide as a group and circle those details.

Information on diabetes	
Definitions	- diabetics: people with diabetes who have too much sugar in their blood - insulin regulates sugar in the blood - pancreas: the organ that produces insulin - Type 1 diabetes: the body doesn't produce enough insulin - Type 2 diabetes: the body cannot properly use insulin
Examples and statistics	- over 340 million people in the world have diabetes - majority of diabetes cases are Type 2 - 80% of deaths from diabetes occur in low-income and middle-income countries
Other information	- most people acquire diabetes as adults, but it can also occur in children - symptoms: extreme thirst, increased hunger, weight loss - prevention: eat fruits and vegetables, exercise, keep a healthy body weight - treatment of severe cases: insulin in pills or injections

C. With your group, write an informational brochure on diabetes. Use your list of questions from activity A and the information from activity B.

D. Share your informational brochure with the class. As a class, discuss these questions.

1. How did you organize the information from the chart?

2. Does your brochure use subheadings or lists? Did they make the information easier to read?

3. Is all of the information in your brochure useful for the general public? How?

Independent Writing

A. Choose a public health issue to become the topic of an informational brochure. It can be an issue that you care about or one you have read about. Staying healthy and preventing illness is also a possible topic.

Health issue: _____

B. What questions does the brochure need to answer? List them below.

Question 1: _____

Question 2: _____

Question 3: _____

Question 4: _____

Question 5: _____

C. Create an extended definition to explain the issue. Follow the steps below as a guide.

1. Define the issue. How does the dictionary define it? What other key terms and definitions help explain it?

_____

_____

2. Give background information. How did it become a problem?

_____

_____

3. Describe its effects. What does it do to the body?

_____

_____

4. Give practical guidelines. How do you contract it? How is it treated? How can people prevent it?

_____

_____

5. Give examples and statistics. How many people does it affect? Is it isolated to certain environments or is it widespread?

_____

_____

D. The words and phrases below are often used to discuss health issues. Write a sentence from the writing model on pages 46–68 that uses each word or phrase. Some of the terms may appear in the same sentence in the writing model.

VOCABULARY TIP

The health and medical fields use specific words and phrases to discuss health-related topics. Using these words shows that you are knowledgeable about these issues.

1. to treat: _Antibiotics are used to treat bacterial infections._

2. spread from: _____

3. contract: _____

4. symptoms: _____

5. prevent/prevention: _____

6. spread of: _____

E. Plan how you will organize the information in your brochure. Answer these questions as a guide.

1. What main ideas can be made into subheadings?

_____

2. What information can be put into bulleted lists?

_____

3. What information can be provided in numbered steps?

_____

F. Write an informational brochure about your health issue. Include the information most relevant to your audience and use the questions you developed. Format the brochure so that the most important information is easy to read. In your writing, use target vocabulary from page 45 and include words and phrases from activity D.

A. Read your informational brochure. Answer the questions below, and make revisions to your brochure as needed.

1. Check (✓) the information you included in your informational brochure.

   ☐ a definition   ☐ description of who is at risk

   ☐ background information   ☐ symptoms and effects

   ☐ description of how the illness   ☐ examples or statistics
   is contracted

                                           ☐ ways to prevent and treat it

2. Look at the information you did not include. Would adding that information make your brochure more effective at educating readers on the issue?

Grammar for Editing   Verbs in Adjective Clauses

1. The relative pronouns *that, which,* or *who* in an adjective clause represent the nouns they describe in the independent clause. Check that the verb in an adjective clause agrees with the noun that it describes in the independent clause.

       noun   verb
   The doctors <u>*who work in that clinic*</u> are experts on allergy care.

2. When an adjective clause includes a noun that appears after *that, which,* or *who,* the verb in the adjective clause must agree with that noun.

               noun verb
   The hospital <u>*that my parents go to*</u> is following strict safety regulations.

B. Check the language in your informational brochure. Revise and edit as needed.

Language Checklist
☐   I used target words in my brochure.
☐   I used words and phrases that are common in the medical and health fields.
☐   I used adjective clauses to define or describe nouns.
☐   I used verbs correctly in adjective clauses.

C. Check your informational brochure again. Repeat activities A and B.

Self-Assessment Review: Go back to page 45 and reassess your

knowledge of the target vocabulary. How has your understanding of the words changed? What words do you feel most comfortable using now?

UNIT

5

Scenes That Inspire

In this unit, you will

> analyze film reviews and learn how they are used to inform and persuade.
> use persuasive writing.
> increase your understanding of the target academic words for this unit.

WRITING SKILLS

> Evaluative Language
> Supporting a Point of View
> **GRAMMAR** Shifting Verb Tenses

Self-Assessment

Think about how well you know each target word, and check (✓) the appropriate column. I have...

TARGET WORDS	never seen the word before.	heard or seen the word but am not sure what it means.	heard or seen the word and understand what it means.	used the word confidently in *either* speaking or writing.
AWL				
attain				
🔑 contrast				
🔑 debate				
displace				
enhance				
eventual				
extract				
🔑 imply				
prohibit				
🔑 somewhat				
subsequent				
🔑 sum				
🔑 tape				
virtual				

🔑 Oxford 3000™ keywords

Building Knowledge

Read these questions. Discuss your answers in a small group.

1. Do you read reviews before you see a movie? Why, or why not?

2. What do you want to know from a movie review?

3. Do you prefer to read reviews written by professional movie critics or reviews written by movie audience members? Why?

Writing Models

A film review summarizes a film, analyzes elements such as the acting, script, or camera work, and argues an opinion of the film. Read two film reviews.

REVIEW 1
THE BLIND SIDE:
MORE THAN A GAME

The Blind Side starts with a **taped** clip from an American football game. The voice on the **tape** is that of actress Sandra Bullock, who plays Leigh Anne in the movie. "There's a moment of orderly silence
5 before a football play begins. Players are in position, linemen are frozen, and anything's possible," says Leigh Anne. This opening scene **implies** that you are about to see a motivating[1] story about football. And that is **somewhat** true. But to **extract** this as the only
10 meaning would be an error. Life is the playing field in *The Blind Side*, and anything is possible. Directed by John Lee Hancock, this drama carries an inspiring message about family, hard work, and determination. The element of football only **enhances** this story about a homeless teenager who is adopted by a
15 wealthy family and succeeds despite his difficult start in life. While Leigh Anne, rather than the central character, provides the film's main voice, the movie still has enough emotional impact to be a winner with any viewer.

Leigh Anne welcomes Michael into her family.

---

[1] *motivating:* making people want to do or accomplish something

The script is based on the true story of Michael Oher, a teenager living in
Tennessee. Through flashbacks, we see scenes from Michael's past and
learn that he bounced around from home to home and school to school as
a child. The first part of the movie shows Michael at a new school on the
opposite side of town. He is **displaced** from all that he knew. We see his
face, his big and vulnerable[2] eyes, and his oversized height. We watch
Michael sitting silently in classrooms, friendless and alone. **Subsequently**,
Leigh Anne sees him walking in the rain. "Do you have a place to stay
tonight? Don't you dare lie to me," she orders, and Michael answers honestly.
She welcomes him into her family and, throughout the movie, pushes him to
attain confidence and develop new skills. For example, when Michael is
prohibited from playing football until he improves his grades, Leigh Anne
hires a tutor for him. While some critics argue that Leigh Anne's character is
too unemotional, Sandra Bullock won a well-deserved Academy Award for her
portrayal of the tough mother in this movie.

Like Hancock's other sports film, *The Rookie*, it is clear from around the
midpoint of *The Blind Side* that the story will **eventually** reach a happy ending.
However, this true story is so remarkable that the movie is still as exciting as
watching a favorite sports game. You'll cheer just as much, and your heart will
lift as high and fall as hard while you watch Michael struggle. In the end,
you'll realize that the story is about much more than a game. It's the tale of
how a family changed one young man's life. I recommend this film for
everyone, sports fans and drama fans alike.

---

[2] *vulnerable:* easy to attack, hurt, or defeat; open to danger

The movie is as exciting as a football game.

REVIEW 2
THE TURTLE: A WORLD IN NEED OF SAVING

The short movie *The Turtle*, filmed for the United Arab Emirates area at a World's Fair, won several international awards. It's rare for a film that lasts less than 15 minutes and whose starring actor is an unknown 14-year-old to
5 receive such attention. However, it's also rare for a message to be expressed so beautifully. The film is a contribution to the **debate** about environmental protection, arguing that technological development does not have to hurt the environment. *The Turtle* celebrates
10 the human achievement of building a large city in the desert and shows how we can save animals with easy changes to our behavior. The movie supports this idea through a simple, appealing story that viewers of any age and from any country will understand.

Sea turtles live in the Gulf near the United Arab Emirates.

15 In the opening scene, the viewer experiences the quiet, dreamlike quality of being submerged[3] in the dark depths of the ocean. A young boy, played by Ahmed al-Dahouri, smiles and swims toward a sea turtle as a plastic bag waves in the water close by. And suddenly the beauty is gone. The same boy wakes up to the laughter of his classmates. His teacher tells him, "No one's ever learned anything
20 by dreaming." In **contrast**, the boy's father tells him, "A dream is the breath of an idea. The greatest miracle we have is that a single idea from the human mind can transform the world." The boy acts on his dream and works with his classmates to educate the public on how plastic bags are dangerous for sea turtles. Finally, the boys help pass a law to eliminate plastic bags in the United
25 Arab Emirates.

In **sum**, *The Turtle* tells the story of a boy's dream to save turtles by working with people in the city he loves. It captures the beauty of the world through a child's eyes. How does it accomplish so much in so little time? **Virtually** every scene makes a simple plea[4] for the environment. From the crystal blue of the
30 sea, the gleaming harbor, the jagged line of the mountains, the soft sands of the desert to the towering lights of the city, the world has never looked more like something worth saving.

---

[3] *submerged:* completely under water
[4] *plea:* a strong request

WRITING SKILL   Evaluative Language

LEARN

In a review, you evaluate the film or book for your reader. You also provide a summary of the story. Evaluate the film or book by giving a summary and then describing your point of view, or how you felt while watching or reading that part:

summary   evaluation

The audience can hear what the main character is thinking. This helped me understand the character, but it also made the story feel less real.

Finally, include your overall opinion, what value you feel the story offers, and who you think would most enjoy it:

The story is serious, but there's enough humor to keep the movie happy. This movie is a good way for children to learn about the environment, so I recommend it to families.

APPLY

A. Read the statements below. Write *S* for summary and *P* for point of view. Write *B* if the statement contains both.

_P_ 1. Life is the playing field in *The Blind Side*, and anything is possible.

___ 2. The script is based on the true story of Michael Oher.

___ 3. It captures the beauty of the world through a child's eyes.

___ 4. Subsequently, Leigh Anne sees him walking in the rain.

___ 5. However, this true story is so remarkable that the movie is still as exciting as watching a favorite sports game.

___ 6. While Leigh Anne, rather than the central character, provides the film's main voice, the movie still has enough emotional impact to be a winner with any viewer.

B. Combine each pair of statements below to create a sentence that contains both a summary and an evaluation.

1. The book is set in the 17ᵗʰ century. Events from history are boring.

   The book is set in the 17ᵗʰ century, and to me it was like a boring history book.

2. The script is funny. It is about two friends traveling to their childhood hometown.

   _____

3. Many scenes take place in the Japanese countryside. The beautiful landscape makes those scenes feel peaceful.

   _____

4. The story is about a large family. Having so many characters was confusing.

   _____

Analyze

A. Read the two film reviews on pages 62–64 again and check (✓) what is included in the chart below. What is in both reviews? What is only in one? Compare your answers with a partner.

	The Blind Side Review	*The Turtle* Review
Description of opening scene	✓	✓
Description of the story's ending		
Description of how scenes look		
Description of characters' appearance		
Comparison to other films		
Statement of message or moral		
Awards the movie has received		
Statement about what other critics have written		

B. Discuss the questions below with a partner. Share your answers with the class.

1. a. Look at the title of each review. Does it contain the title of the movie?

   b. How is the phrase after the colon in each review title related to the review?

2. a. How does it affect the reader when a review includes the story's ending?

   b. Do you think that reviews should reveal the ending?

3. a. When the writer describes characters or scenes, is he stating summary, point of view, or both?

   b. How do these descriptions help readers decide whether or not to see the movie?

4. a. How does it affect the reader to learn that a film or book has won awards?

   b. Should reviews mention a story's awards and other critical attention?

5. a. Should a review state the story's message?

   b. Can a story have value without a clear moral?

C. In both reviews, underline the summary phrases and circle the phrases that express the writer's point of view.

D. Discuss these questions with a partner.

1. Do summary and opinion phrases occur in the same paragraph or separately?

2. Read only the opinion phrases. Is the review as effective without any summary?

3. One review includes a rebuttal, or response to other critics. Does the rebuttal strengthen the writer's argument?

Vocabulary Activities | STEP I: Word Level

A. Fill in the missing words in the chart below. Check the spelling and meaning of the new words in your dictionary.

Word Form Chart			
Noun	**Verb**	**Adjective**	**Adverb**
attainment	attain	*attainable*	_____
	displace		_____
	enhance		_____
_____	_____	eventual	
_____	_____	subsequent	
_____		virtual	

B. Use one of the word forms from activity A to complete the sentences below. Change verb endings as needed. Use the words in parentheses for help.

The problem with basing a movie on a book is that it's _____*virtually*_____

(1. almost)

impossible to make everyone happy. Everyone has a different idea of

how the characters look and sound. In addition, filmmakers often hope

to _____ status and make money from the movie. They try to

(2. achieve or gain)

_____ the movie with special effects such as fast car races or

(3. improve)

explosions. They change dialogs, cut scenes, and end up _____

(4. replacing)

the original story to make it fit into two hours. _____ the story

(5. In the end)

becomes something else. However, the _____ result, while

(6. following)

different, isn't always bad.

C. Answer the questions with the correct target word from the box below. Use a dictionary if needed.

attain	debate	displace	eventual
somewhat	subsequent	sum	virtual

1. Which word is used to discuss an amount of money and also is used after the preposition *in* to introduce a main idea? _____ *sum* _____

2. Which word is a verb meaning "to force someone or something to move from the usual or correct place"? _____

3. Which two words share the same ending because they are the same part of speech? _____ _____

4. Which target word is a formal way of saying "coming after"? _____

5. What target word could replace the circled word in this sentence: I will get my degree next year. _____

6. Which verb means "to argue" and collocates with the adverbs *seriously, thoroughly, fiercely, hotly, openly,* and *publicly*? _____

7. Which adverb combines two short words and means "a little"? _____

In mathematics, the noun *sum* refers to "the answer you get from adding two numbers together." As a verb, *sum* is used with the preposition *up*. To *sum up* is "to describe main ideas in a few words."

> To **sum up** our discussion, we're going to increase the film's budget.

CORPUS

D. The words *sum, contrast, debate, extract,* and *tape* have the same form as both nouns and verbs. Underline the target word in each sentence. Write *N* for noun or *V* for verb. Then ask and answer the questions with a partner.

__V__ 1. What color <u>contrasts</u> with blue?

____ 2. What contrast does the review of *The Turtle* present?

____ 3. What are some issues that government officials often debate?

____ 4. Where do you think the movie *The Blind Side* was taped?

____ 5. Sum up your favorite movie. What is it about?

____ 6. Have you ever enjoyed an extract from a novel, but then not liked the full book when you read it?

E. When you *imply* something, you don't say exactly what you mean. You hint at it. Match the statements with what they imply. Then write a sentence naming each implication.

_b_ 1. I need to get a warmer coat.　　　　　　　a. not excited

___ 2. I'm somewhat interested in seeing the movie.　　b. cold

___ 3. You could enhance the song by speeding it up.　　c. very smart

___ 4. She is so young to attain a second degree!　　　d. too slow

i. _He's implying that he's cold._ _____

ii. _____

iii. _____

iv. _____

When you *contrast* two things, you "show the differences between them." *Contrast* can be used with different prepositions as a noun or verb.

The movie version of the story **contrasts** *dramatically* <u>with</u> *the book version.*

<u>In</u> **contrast** <u>to</u> *the book, the movie has a happy ending.*

There is a **contrast** <u>between</u> *what the character says and what she does.*

CORPUS

F. Write sentences contrasting the items in each pair. Use *contrasts with*, *in contrast to*, and *contrast between*.

1. bus, car

   One contrast between cars and buses is that buses can carry many more people.

2. pencil, computer

   _____

3. movie, book

   _____

4. running in a gym, running outside

   _____

G. Your friend has asked you whether or not he should study abroad for a year. Write arguments for each side of the question. Use *contrast*, *eventually*, and *sum*.

Reasons he should study abroad for a year	Reasons he should not study abroad for a year
1. *He'll make friends from other cultures.*	2. *In contrast, he might be lonely.*
3. _____	4. _____
5. _____	6. _____

H. Write a sentence to state what might be prohibited at each place.

1. swimming pool *Diving and running are often prohibited at swimming pools.*

2. movie theater _____

3. restaurant _____

4. high school _____

5. park _____

Grammar Shifting Verb Tenses

In reviews, writers use the present tense to discuss a book or movie.

> *The Blind Side* <u>starts</u> with a taped clip from an American football game.

The present tense is also used to state an argument or opinion.

> Life <u>is</u> the playing field in *The Blind Side*, and anything <u>is</u> possible.

Verb tenses shift to match the events in the story. Anything happening *now* for the characters of the story is also happening *now* for the review writer. Use past tense verbs to discuss events that occurred in the fictional *past* for the characters of the story.

> The script <u>is</u> based on the true story of Michael Oher.   discuss the movie

> Leigh Anne <u>hires</u> a tutor for him.   what the movie is showing now

> He <u>bounced</u> around from home to home as a child.   events from the character's past

A. Complete this book review with the appropriate tense of each verb in parentheses. Use the present tense to discuss events in the book and the reviewer's opinion. Use the past tense to discuss Stephen Venables's life before he wrote to the book.

Stephen Venables _____was_____ the first British person to climb
                        (1. be)

Mt. Everest without an oxygen tank, and his autobiography, *Higher Than*

the Eagle Soars, _____ more like an adventure novel than a true
                        (2. seem)

story. The book _____ stories about his exciting and dangerous
                    (3. include)

climbs in Peru, Nepal, and other places around the world. "Mountaineers

are expected to explain themselves," Venables _____, and in
                                                    (4. begin)

the book he _____ to explain why he _____ jobs and
                (5. try)   (6. leave)

almost _____ in order to climb mountains. And his explanation
            (7. die)

_____ successful. I _____ this book even to readers who
    (8. be)   (9. recommend)

have never seen a mountain, because through Venables's honest and often

funny writing, we all _____ the top of Mt. Everest.
                        (10. experience)

B. Practice summarizing and evaluating a story you know well. Shift verb tenses to match what you are writing about.

1. Name the story and the main character.

   _____

2. Give background information about the main character by describing his or her life before the time of the story.

   _____

3. Tell the story's main message or the theme it focuses on.

   _____

4. Describe an event in the story that connects to the main theme or message.

   _____

5. Who would you recommend the story to?

   _____

WRITING SKILL Supporting a Point of View

LEARN

When writing a film or book review, support your opinion with examples from the story.

1. Direct quotes from the film strengthen your argument:

    Leigh Anne's character is tough. "Don't you dare lie to me," she orders.

2. Details of the setting and filming or writing style show how you experienced the story:

    The film often shows Michael standing near other characters, which reminds us how much taller he is than everyone else.

Writing techniques can also make your argument stronger.

3. Writing a question and then answering it draws attention to your main point:

    Why has the book been so popular? Because people want to be like the main character.

4. Using the pronoun *we*, instead of *I* or *you*, can help your readers feel that they are experiencing the story with you:

    By the end of the book, we feel like we have been on a long trip.

APPLY

A. The writers of the reviews on pages 62–64 support their arguments in different ways. Check (✓) the review that uses each technique.

	The Blind Side Review	*The Turtle* Review
direct quotes or dialog from the movie	✓	✓
question and answer		
description of a character, setting, or filming technique		
use of the pronoun *we*		

B. Work with a partner. Find this opinion statement in the review of *The Blind Side* on pages 62–63. Fill in the ways that the writer supports his point of view.

Review of *The Blind Side*	
Opinion statement	While Leigh Anne, rather than the central character, provides the film's main voice, the movie still has enough emotional impact to be a winner with any viewer.
Quote	*"Do you have a place to stay tonight? Don't you dare lie to me," she orders, and Michael answers honestly.*
Description of characters	

C. Work with a partner. Find this opinion statement in the review of *The Turtle* on page 64. Then list the ways that the writer supports this opinion and write examples from the review.

Review of *The Turtle*	
Opinion statement	The movie argues for this compromise through a simple, appealing story that viewers of any age and from any country will understand.
Description of a scene	
_____	
_____	

D. Circle the pronouns *we*, *you*, and *your* in the movie reviews. Discuss the questions below with a partner.

1. Where does the word *we* occur? Could the writer have used *I* instead?

2. How does the writer's decision to use *we* change the way the sentences affect readers?

3. When are the pronouns *you* or *your* used? What effect does it have on the reader?

4. What effect does it have when the writer asks and then answers a question?

Collaborative Writing

A. In your opinion, what are the most important aspects of a story? Rank the following. Use *1* for the most important and *5* for the least important.

____ the characters

____ the moral or message

____ the plot

____ whether the story is true

____ the setting: vivid description or visually appealing scenes

B. Which aspects of a story did you rank *1* and *2*? Find two other students with the same top two aspects as you. Choose one aspect you agree is the most important.

C. With your group, write a paragraph about why the aspect you chose in activity B is the most important. Complete the sentences below as a guide.

The most important aspect of a story is _____.

_____ is important because it makes the story _____.

Why is _____ the most important? Because _____.

_____ helps us, as readers, to _____.

D. Share your paragraph with the class. Discuss these questions as a class.

1. How persuasive were the arguments?
2. Did any of the arguments change your mind?

Independent Writing

A. What is a movie or story you can review? Think of a movie you have seen or a story you have read recently.

B. Answer the questions below to organize your summary.

1. What is the title? How does it connect to the story?

_____

2. Who are the main characters? What should your reader know about them?

_____

3. What are the key events in the story?

_____

4. Do you want to tell the ending in your review? Why, or why not?

_____

C. Answer the questions below to help you evaluate the movie or story.

1. What importance does the movie or story have? Does it share a lesson? Does it give an important insight? Explain.

_____

2. Write a sentence that clearly states your overall opinion of the movie or story.

_____

VOCABULARY TIP

Avoid using intensifiers like *very, extremely,* or *really* when writing about your opinion. Instead, use words that have their own strong meaning.

For example, rather than writing *very interesting*, use the word *fascinating*.

D. Write examples from the story that support your opinion. Answer the questions below and fill in the chart as a guide.

1. What quotes from the story are most connected to your opinion statement?

2. List additional examples below that support your argument. You may describe a character, describe a scene, or comment on the writing or filming style.

Supporting examples	
Example 1:	
Example 2:	
Example 3:	

E. Use persuasive writing techniques in your review. Follow the steps below as a guide.

1. Write sentences about how you felt while watching the movie or reading the story. Use *we* instead of *I*.

_____

_____

2. What aspect of the movie or story best supports your opinion? Write a question about that aspect. Then write an answer to the question using your point of view.

_____

_____

F. Write your movie or story review. Use your summary from activity B, evaluation from activity C, and supporting arguments and writing techniques from activities D and E. In your writing, use the target vocabulary words from page 61.

A. Read your review. Answer the questions below, and make revisions to your review as needed.

1. Check (✓) the information you included in the review.

   ☐ summary   ☐ quotations or dialog

   ☐ opinion statement   ☐ persuasive writing techniques

   ☐ description of scenes or characters

2. Look at the information you did not include. Would adding that information help support your point of view?

Grammar for Editing | Subject-Verb Agreement

Check the subject-verb agreement of each sentence in your review.

1. First, identify the subject of the clause. Then make sure the verb matches the subject.

          S   V

   The Blind Side starts with a taped clip from an American football game.

   The title of a book or movie is considered third person singular. The third person singular form of a verb ends in –s. Also, notice that titles are written in italics.

2. Remember that _it's_ is a contraction of _it is_.

   It's rare for a film that lasts less than 15 minutes to receive so much attention.

3. Check the subject and verb in each clause of the sentence.

                  S   V   S   V   S   V

   While some critics argue that Leigh Anne is too unemotional, Sandra Bullock won a well-deserved Academy Award for her portrayal of the tough mother in this movie.

B. Check the language in your review. Revise and edit as needed.

Language Checklist
☐ I used target words in my review.
☐ I used the present tense to give a summary or argue a point and the past tense to discuss events in the characters' past.
☐ I used verbs that agree with the subjects in my sentences.
☐ I used vivid adjectives when evaluating a story.

C. Check your review again. Repeat activities A and B.

Self-Assessment Review: Go back to page 61 and reassess your knowledge of the target vocabulary. How has your understanding of the words changed? What words do you feel most comfortable using now?

UNIT 6

Reinvent, Redesign, Reimagine

In this unit, you will

> analyze an editorial and learn how it is used to present a position about community issues.
> use problem/solution writing.
> increase your understanding of the target academic words for this unit.

WRITING SKILLS

> Formal Register
> Proposing Solutions
> **GRAMMAR** Non-Defining Adjective Clauses

Self-Assessment

Think about how well you know each target word, and check (✓) the appropriate column. I have…

TARGET WORDS	never seen the word before.	heard or seen the word but am not sure what it means.	heard or seen the word and understand what it means.	used the word confidently in *either* speaking or writing.
AWL				
accommodate				
assemble				
🔑 collapse				
facilitate				
🔑 license				
ratio				
reinforce				
restrain				
🔑 stable				
sustain				
🔑 technical				
🔑 technique				
utilize				
violate				

🔑 Oxford 3000™ keywords

Building Knowledge

Read these questions. Discuss your answers in a small group.

1. Describe a downtown or city center that you find attractive. What do you like about it?

2. Have you ever read an editorial? What was it about?

3. If you were writing an editorial, what would you write about?

Writing Model

An editorial is a letter that someone writes to a publication, such as a newsletter, so that his or her opinion can reach a wide audience. Read this editorial that proposes a solution to a problem in a city's downtown area.

A Sustainable Plan for Downtown from a City Engineer's Point of View

I attended the recent city council meeting about the redesign of Newton's downtown area. Especially controversial, as I'm sure readers know, is the plan to eliminate 45–55 of the mature trees that line the
5 largest streets. Most people **assembled** at the meeting were opposed to the tree removal. By my estimate, the **ratio** of speakers against the plan to those in favor was six-to-one.

However, people misunderstand the problem. The
10 problem is not that the city planners and store owners don't like trees. As a city engineer with over 11 years of experience, I can assure you that the problem is that the trees are the wrong kind and they're in the wrong place. Maple trees, which are the most common trees on Butler
15 Street and Green Street, are especially bad. Their roots have broken through the sidewalks in many places. Cracked pavement **violates** city safety codes because sidewalks **accommodate** pedestrians (including young children and the elderly) and strollers. Someone who tripped and fell could **sustain** injuries. The sidewalks obviously have to be repaired, but damaging the roots could cause the entire
20 tree to **collapse**. Leaving the roots endangers infrastructure[1] such as water lines.

A cracked sidewalk in downtown Newton

---

[1] *infrastructure:* basic systems and services needed in a community such as buildings, transportation, and water and power supplies.

Eventually roots can spread under the streets in one direction and crack and damage the pavement, and grow under the foundations[2] of buildings in the other direction. This could cost thousands of dollars, both in city street repairs and to business owners. Yet cutting part of the roots means that the tree might not be
25 able to **sustain** itself.

Maples grow fast, which is why they were **utilized** in the first place, but their rapid growth results in brittle[3] wood that isn't **stable**. Strong storm winds bring down these weak branches, which could injure citizens. It's true that there are **techniques** for **reinforcing** weak branches, but they're difficult, expensive, and
30 unattractive.

The oak trees aren't much better. Their large seeds attract squirrels, which then try to nest in the roofs and walls of local shops. Store owners, by law, aren't allowed to trap or kill these animals. Instead, they have to call **licensed** exterminators,[4] who are costly. Oaks have wide shady branches, which look lovely
35 in summer, but also block drivers' views of other cars and cyclists. This creates hazardous conditions at some corners.

However, the main solution proposed—removing all the trees—also isn't the best. Beauty is important in a community, too, and trees are an essential part of what makes the downtown area attractive.

40 The solution I advocate[5] is this. First, remove the problem trees. Then bring in different trees such as ginkos or Chinese elms, which are ideal for cities because they're easy to **sustain**. They're **stable** and fast-growing, they resist pollution, and they don't **utilize** much water, so they don't need much attention.

But instead of attempting some **technical** solution to keep tree roots from
45 damaging the infrastructure, put the trees in planter boxes. The boxes will **restrain** the roots, which will also keep the trees from growing too large. The containers could be relocated, too, to **accommodate** events such as merchant sidewalk sales and parades or to **facilitate** pedestrian traffic flow. Make it a **violation** to damage the trees or to move them without a **license** and **reinforce**
50 the rules by posting signs near the trees. Keep a sensible **ratio** of trees to open spaces.

I urge the city council to implement a **sustainable** plan for the future. Plant trees, yes, but plant them sensibly so that future generations of residents can enjoy them—and our municipal[6] streets and retail outlets—for years to come.

55 Martin Bradford, Municipal Engineer

---

[2] *foundation:* the solid underground base of a building
[3] *brittle:* easily broken or fragile
[4] *exterminator:* a person whose job is to kill or remove certain insects and animals from buildings
[5] *advocate:* to support something publicly
[6] *municipal:* related to a town, city, or district that has its own local government

LEARN

In writing, *register* means the type of language that you use in a certain context. For example, if you are sending a friend a message on your phone, you probably use a very informal register. You might use short words, abbreviations, and symbols. If you are writing an academic paper, you will use a formal register.

The editorial on pages 78–79 uses a formal register because the writer wants to establish himself as an authority. He uses language to sound well-informed. Here are some features of formal register that you can use:

1. More technical or sophisticated vocabulary

   mature trees   instead of   *old trees*

2. Single-word verbs instead of phrasal verbs

   attend a meeting   instead of   *go to a meeting*

3. Confident language that shows you are presenting facts

   The problem is   instead of   *In my opinion, the problem is*

APPLY

A. Read the informal phrases below. Then find the phrases in the editorial on pages 78–79 that have the same meaning but are more formal. Write them here.

1. people walk on the sidewalks

   sidewalks accommodate pedestrians

2. The answer I like is this.

   _____

3. I think you should make it a crime to hurt the trees.

   _____

4. our city streets and stores

   _____

B. Work with a partner. Rewrite the sentences in a formal register. Then discuss where the sentences could appear in the editorial on pages 78–79.

1. I think some people who work for the city should plant the trees.

   _____

2. It's hard to drive in the fall when a lot of leaves fall all over the road.

   _____

3. In my opinion, these animals are not very clean and could even be sick, which might be bad for people who live and do things near them.

   _____

Analyze

A. Read the editorial on pages 78–79 again. Answer the questions below with a partner.

1. What problem does the editorial focus on?

   _____

2. How does the writer establish himself as an expert on this problem?

   _____

3. What solution does the writer propose?

   _____

B. What is the purpose of each paragraph in the editorial? Write a brief description. Compare your answers with a partner.

Paragraph 1: _to give background information about the problem_____

Paragraph 2: _____

Paragraph 3: _____

Paragraph 4: _____

Paragraph 5: _____

Paragraph 6: _____

Paragraph 7: _____

Paragraph 8: _____

C. Answer these questions in a small group.

1. Who do you think is the writer's intended audience? Who is he trying

   to persuade? _____

2. Is there any other information he could have included to strengthen his argument?

   _____

3. In some formal registers, the first person pronouns *I* and *we* are not used. Why do you think the writer uses them in the editorial?

   _____

D. Write an example from the editorial on pages 78–79 of the writer using a formal register to accomplish these purposes:

- persuade others to take a course of action

  I urge the city council to implement a sustainable plan for the future.

- establish himself as an authority

  _____

- sound intelligent and well-informed

  _____

Vocabulary Activities STEP I: Word Level

A. Complete the chart below with the correct forms of the target words in the box. Use a dictionary to check your answers.

accommodation	assemble	sustainability
technique	unsustainable	utilize

Word Form Chart			
Noun	**Verb**	**Adjective**	**Adverb**
accommodation	accommodate	_____	_____
assembly		_____	_____
	_____	sustainable	_____
	_____	_____	_____
utility		_____	_____

B. Check (✓) the occupations or activities below that might require a license. Compare your answers with a partner.

_✓_ 1. driving a bus   ___ 4. engineer

___ 2. teacher   ___ 5. being a parent

___ 3. riding a bicycle   ___ 6. owning a restaurant

C. Replace the words in parentheses with the correct form of a target word from the box. You will use one word twice.

accommodate	assemble	collapse	facilitate
reinforce	stable	technical	utilize

In August 2010, part of a copper and gold mine in northern Chile

_____collapsed_____, trapping 33 workers almost five kilometers underground.
   (1. caved in)

Individuals and groups from several countries offered their _____
                         (2. specialized)

expertise to Chile to _____ the rescue of the trapped miners.
          (3. make happen)

The rescue team _____ huge drills to dig through the ground.
        (4. used)

They were concerned that drilling could cause another area of rock to

_____. But the rock remained _____ and the drill
   (5. fall apart)   (6. steady)

reached the miners. Other technicians had _____ a capsule to carry
                     (7. built)

the men, one by one, up the newly drilled hole. The capsule had to be wide

enough to _____ a man, but narrow enough to slide through the
       (8. hold)

hole the rescue team had drilled. The capsule also had to be strong; the roof

was _____ to protect the person inside from falling rocks. All 33
   (9. strengthened)

miners made the journey up through the earth to safety.

Vocabulary Activities STEP II: Sentence Level

D. Read each description. Then explain the ratio. Use the word *ratio* in your answer.

1. There are four walkers for every bicyclist in this city.

   The ratio of walkers to bicyclists is four-to-one.

2. There are four computers and twelve students in this class.

   _____

3. Two out of four people that study engineering get jobs in another field.

   _____

4. For every park in the city, there are 400 residents.

   _____

Restrain can be used to discuss people or things. To *restrain* is "to keep someone or something under control or to prevent someone or something from doing something." The noun form is *restraint*.

*The police used barricades to **restrain** the crowd.*

*When you live in the city, you accept certain space **restraints**. Most people I know don't have extra bedrooms or unused space.*

E. Read each item in the list. Write a sentence using each item and *restrain* or *restraint*. Discuss your answers with a partner.

1. a seat belt

   A seat belt will restrain your body safely in a car accident.

2. self-control

   _____

3. a budget

   _____

4. handcuffs

   _____

5. a fence

   _____

When you *violate* something, you "refuse to obey a law or agreement." *Violate* is a transitive verb that takes an object, and the object is usually the law or agreement that has been broken.

*She **violated the terms** of the contract by missing her deadlines.*

Violate can also mean "to disturb something or not to respect something." In both senses, *violate* indicates a negative action.

*Wanda is no longer speaking to Lila. Lila **violated her trust** when she posted the details of their argument online.*

Violation is a noun and refers to the act of *violating*.

F. Read each scenario. Work with a partner to identify the violation and the person or thing that is violated.

1. The speed limit is 55 miles per hour and a car races past at 65 miles per hour.

   Violation: _driving too fast_

   Person or thing violated: _speed limit_

2. Julia was upset about her day and wrote about it in her journal. When she left the house, her younger sister read her journal without her permission.

   Violation: _____

   Person or thing violated: _____

3. Building codes require two fire exits on each floor of a building. The designs for a new office building include only one fire exit on each floor.

   Violation: _____

   Person or thing violated: _____

4. City law requires property owners to keep their walkways clean. Mr. Sayed never removes the leaves and dust from his walkway.

   Violation: _____

   Person or thing violated: _____

G. A *technique* is a method of doing something. Use the word *technique* to write about your methods for doing the following tasks. Share your sentences with a partner.

1. write an essay

   My technique is to write an outline first, then the whole essay.

2. learn a new sport

   _____

3. shop for clothing

   _____

4. choose where to go on vacation

   _____

The verb *facilitate* means "to make an action or process possible or easier."

*A good leader **facilitates** change and growth.*

The noun *facilitator* is "a person who helps someone do something more easily."

*Every group should assign a **facilitator** to keep the project moving.*

CORPUS

H. What would help the following happen more quickly or easily? Write sentences using a form of *facilitate* or *facilitator*.

1. studying

   A quiet room facilitates studying.

2. cooking a meal

3. traveling in a new city

4. assembling furniture

5. organizing volunteers to clean up a park

Grammar Non-Defining Adjective Clauses

Like adjectives, adjective clauses describe nouns. Non-defining adjective clauses give additional, non-essential information about a noun.

               noun   adjective clause
They have to call licensed exterminators, *who are costly*.

The adjective clause above describes the cost of exterminators, but that information isn't necessary to understand the sentence. You could end the sentence after *exterminators*.

Begin a non-defining adjective clause with *who* to refer to people and *which* to refer to objects. Do not use *that*. *That* is only used for defining adjective clauses. Place a comma before the relative pronoun.

Although adjective clauses cannot form a sentence on their own, they do contain a subject and a verb. The relative pronoun is the subject.

             subject   verb
The boxes will restrain the roots, *which will also keep the trees from growing too large*.

A. Read the paragraph. Put brackets ([ ]) around each non-defining adjective clause. Then correct the errors, including incorrect relative pronouns, clause structure, or comma use.

                                     which

The city's planning department, [~~that~~ has been working on the Heritage Park redesign project], announced that improvements can be made without removing any existing trees. Heritage Park which is known for its beautiful and stable oak and maple trees, will soon be a sports and recreation destination for residents. Improvements include a new playground, playing fields with lighting for night games, and public restrooms. New lights will be installed for residents of the neighborhood, which insisted on more lighting for safety.

B. Combine the following sentences into one sentence using a non-defining adjective clause. Use the correct relative pronoun as the subject of the adjective clause.

1. I have experience in creating water purification systems. Creating water purification systems requires mechanical engineering skills and knowledge about water.

   I have experience in creating water purification systems, which requires

   mechanical engineering skills and knowledge about water.

2. My new design of the student center provides more open spaces. Open spaces accommodate more student interaction.

   _____

   _____

3. My classmate is helping me revise my editorial. My classmate works on our school newspaper.

   _____

   _____

4. Many people use the phrase *sustainable design. Sustainable design* has become a popular phrase for showing that you are creating environmentally friendly designs.

   _____

   _____

WRITING SKILL Proposing Solutions

LEARN

When writing an editorial, your argument is a solution to a problem. Use signal phrases to show the close relationship between the problem and the solution you are proposing. You may identify one or more issues and propose one solution. Alternately, you may explain one problem and propose several different solutions.

Use these phrases to introduce problems:

- The main problem is (that)

    The main problem is the inadequate foundation.
    The main problem is that the tree roots are cracking the foundation.

- One problem / hazard / danger / difficulty / obstacle is

    One obstacle is the expense of maintaining these trees.

Use these phrases to introduce solutions:

- I propose / advocate / suggest (that)

    I advocate removing the trees.

Words and phrases that show cause and effect are also common when proposing solutions. You can use *because, since, due to, as a result,* and *therefore*:

Don't plant maples, because their branches are too brittle.
Maple trees grow very quickly. As a result, their branches are brittle.

So is an especially useful connector for showing how a solution fits a problem:

Chinese elm trees don't drop many leaves, so they're a good choice near busy streets.

APPLY

A. Write the phrases from the writing model on pages 78–79 that introduce the main problem and solution.

Problem: _____

Solution: _____

B. Read the writing model on pages 78–79 again. Follow the steps below with a partner.

1. Underline two sentences in the editorial that use *so*.

2. Does the writer show cause and effect in these sentences? Discuss how this connects the writer's solution to the problem.

Collaborative Writing

A. Read about Newton City Hall. Discuss the problems with a partner. How serious are they?

Newton City Hall was built in 1848. At that time, people didn't use automobiles for transportation, so no parking garage or parking lot was included. To save money, the building design was very simple: a large rectangle. No wonder Newton City Hall is often called The Big Brick. Also as a cost-cutting measure, not many windows were included, and those that were are quite small. In fact, the measure didn't save money; these days, the cost of electric lighting for the offices has become quite expensive. Finally, some engineers feel that the shallow foundation and poor-quality materials in the exterior walls mean that the building isn't stable.

B. With a partner, choose one or more problems with Newton City Hall that you would like to solve. Write them in the chart below. Then brainstorm solutions.

Newton City Hall	
Problems	**Solutions**

C. With your partner, discuss how you will present the problem(s) and solution(s).

1. How will you organize your editorial?

   a. Will each paragraph be about one problem and solution together?

   b. Or will you write a paragraph about multiple problems and propose solutions in the paragraphs that follow?

2. Will any of your solutions cause additional problems (for example, will any of them require money or resources)? Write those new issues here.

D. Complete the sentences below to use problem/solution phrases.

One issue is that _____.

The main obstacle is _____.

We propose _____.

The best way to solve this problem is _____.

E. With your partner, write an editorial that explains the problem or problems with the City Hall and proposes one or more solutions.

F. Share your editorial with another pair of students. Discuss the questions below together.

1. How were your solutions similar? How were they different?

2. How was your organization of problems and solutions similar? How was it different?

3. What changes would you make to your editorial after seeing the way another pair wrote about the problems with the City Hall?

Independent Writing

A. Think about your town, city, or country. Is there an area that could be improved? Think about a downtown neighborhood or a city square, or a single building such as a school or library.

Place: _____

B. Brainstorm a list of problems that place has that could be solved, such as inadequate parking, poor design, or dangerous conditions.

Problems

C. Choose one or two problems from your list in activity B. Which ones could you solve with enough funding? Make a list of solutions to the problems.

Solutions

D. Complete the sentences below to brainstorm about the audience who will read your editorial.

1. Most of my readers are _____.

2. They already think or know that _____.

E. Add an introduction that will show your reader that you are qualified to give an informed opinion on your topic. Complete the sentences below as a guide:

As a _____, I know that

_____. Through my experience _____,

I have learned that _____. I feel strongly about this topic,

since I am _____.

F. Add a conclusion that asks your readers to take an action. Write who you would like to take the action and what you would like them to do.

People who should take action: _____

What I want them to do: _____

G. Check your editorial to make sure you used a formal register. You may wish to use a dictionary or thesaurus to help you select more formal synonyms for some words.

H. Write your editorial. Use your introduction and conclusion from activities F and G, and organize your problems and solutions from activities B and C. Include details that show you are knowledgeable on the topic, and persuade your audience to take action.

A. Read your editorial. Answer the questions below, and make revisions to your editorial as needed.

1. Check (✓) the information you included in your editorial.

   ☐ introduction   ☐ an explanation of the problem or problems

   ☐ conclusion   ☐ a proposed solution or solutions

   ☐ a call to action

2. Look at the information you did not include. Would adding that information improve your editorial?

Grammar for Editing   Punctuation with Adjective Clauses

Defining adjective clauses, which give information that is necessary for the sentence, do not have commas before the clause.

> This is the building *that will be renovated*.

Non-defining adjective clauses do have a comma before and after the clause.

> Vertecnica, *which is the firm that designed the theater*, has a new downtown office.

To find out whether a clause is defining or non-defining, remove it from the sentence to see if the sentence still makes sense. If the information in the clause is needed in the sentence, it's defining and doesn't require a comma. If the information isn't needed, it's non-defining and should be surrounded by commas.

B. Check the language in your editorial. Revise and edit as needed.

Language Checklist
☐ I used target words in my editorial.
☐ I used formal language in my editorial.
☐ I used non-defining adjective clauses to provide additional information.
☐ I punctuated defining and non-defining adjective clauses correctly.

C. Check your editorial again. Repeat activities A and B.

Self-Assessment Review: Go back to page 77 and reassess your knowledge of the target vocabulary. How has your understanding of the words changed? What words do you feel most comfortable using now?

UNIT 7

The Memories We Keep

In this unit, you will

> analyze a research proposal and learn how it is used in neuroscience.
> use cause-effect writing.
> increase your understanding of the target academic words for this unit.

WRITING SKILLS

> Cause and Effect
> Writing a Hypothesis
> **GRAMMAR** Noun Clauses with *That*

Self-Assessment

Think about how well you know each target word, and check (✓) the appropriate column. I have…

TARGET WORDS	never seen the word before.	heard or seen the word but am not sure what it means.	heard or seen the word and understand what it means.	used the word confidently in *either* speaking or writing.
AWL				
🔑 capable				
consent				
hypothesis				
identical				
implicate				
insight				
🔑 intense				
🔑 interval				
🔑 monitor				
persist				
🔑 publication				
🔑 significant				
🔑 theory				
thesis				

🔑 Oxford 3000™ keywords

Building Knowledge

Read these questions. Discuss your answers in a small group.

1. What is a subject you would like to learn more about?

2. How would you research that subject?

3. What question or questions would you try to answer with your research?

Writing Model

The goal of a research proposal is to gain approval to carry out a research project. Read a research proposal about memory.

Undergraduate Research Proposal: The Relationship between Reflection and Memories

INTRODUCTION

Young adulthood has special **significance** for most people because young people experience many "firsts." They live on their own for the first time and begin to make important decisions for themselves. It may be the
5 first time they travel abroad or get a job. In effect, it is the time when many young people try on[1] the responsibilities of being an adult.

In the 1980s, scientists began seeing a connection between strong memories and this **interval** of time
10 between the teens and the thirties. For some reason, people remember events from this period more strongly than any other period in life. Current research suggests that young adulthood is a **significant** time of life.

However, research has focused on the memories of
15 older individuals. It has not evaluated the thoughts and feelings of young people. I aim to investigate how young adults experience this stage of life.[2] My goal is to see if memory-making is tied to emotions felt during this life stage or if later reflection[3] is what makes this
20 time in life memorable.

We remember events that help form our identity.

---

[1] *try on:* to test something to see if it is suitable to you
[2] *stage of life:* one part in the progress of life
[3] *reflection:* thinking deeply about something

LITERATURE REVIEW

Scientists have tried to understand why people's memories from their twenties are so **intense**. The earliest reports say that it was due to the fact that the brain was younger and more **capable** of storing memories. However, later researchers focus on the type of experiences young people have. They propose[4] that the brain remembers these events because this time is filled with new and interesting experiences. That is, exciting experiences are more memorable. Still other researchers suggest that the brain remembers events that define who we are (Leist et al., 2010). This **theory** suggests that the memories that **persist** are of events that shape identity. These memories support people's values and sense of who they are.

In a 2003 **publication**, Rubin and Berntsen show that people often remember positive memories related to life events. While the events aren't **identical** from person to person, they do represent some of life's **significant** experiences such as marriage or becoming a parent. People recall the major milestones[5] in their lives. Scientists Gluck and Bluck (2007) build on Rubin and Berntsen's **theory**. They propose that the events that produce the strongest memories meet three requirements. They are positive. They allow us to believe we have control over our lives. Lastly, we believe the events will affect our future.

BACKGROUND

I am basing this study on my review of the literature and my personal experience. I am a young adult experiencing many "firsts" right now. Most research focuses on older adults' reflections on their younger selves. Adults look back and see this period of time as positive. They see the events as shaping who they are. I propose interviewing young people. I will look at how they experience events during this time of major change and **intense** emotions. I will assess whether the events are seen as positive while they are experienced. I will also find out if young people consider the events important to their identity.

METHODS

I plan to have 20 students in their freshman year of college keep a journal for the first three weeks of classes. They will **monitor** their feelings and thoughts. Each night they will record memorable events from the day. They will rate each event as positive or negative on a scale of one to ten, ten being the highest positive rating and one being the lowest negative rating. Then they will record whether they think the event will influence them later in life.

Students will sign **consent** forms in advance that will allow me to use their journals. Three months after the journaling, I will survey students on these same factors. I will evaluate if events that the students rate as memorable and positive on the survey were, in fact, described as

Students will record memorable events from the day.

---

[4] *propose:* to suggest something as an explanation, plan, or action
[5] *milestone:* an event representing an important change or transition in life

memorable and positive experiences in the student journals. By comparing the journals with the survey,
60 I aim to gain **insight** into the role of reflection on whether something is positive.

CONCLUSION

Research shows that adults remember the events of their twenties as life-defining. Adults most often describe them as happy moments. However, I
65 propose that the young person is overwhelmed[6] with emotions during this time period. My **hypothesis** is that young people may not experience **significant** events as positive until they reflect on them later. Then they can fit earlier experiences and milestones into a greater understanding of who they are. My **thesis** will test this
70 **hypothesis**. If my **hypothesis** is correct, then the **implication** is that an event may be seen as positive only after time and reflection.

Happy life events can also feel overwhelming.

REFERENCES

Berntsen, D. and D. C. Rubin (2003). Life scripts help to maintain autobiographical memories of highly positive, but not highly negative, events. Memory & Cognition, 31, 1–14.
75 Gluck, J. and S. Bluck (2007). Looking back across the life span: A life story account of the reminiscent bump. Memory & Cognition, 35, 1928–1939.
Leist, A. K., and others (2010). Remembering positive and negative life events. GeroPsych, 23, 137–147.

---

[6] *overwhelmed:* feeling too many strong emotions

WRITING SKILL | Cause and Effect

LEARN

When writing a research proposal, explain what causes and effects you will learn more about through your research. The effect is what happens, and the cause explains why it happens.

Words and phrases that signal cause include *as a result of, because, due to the fact that, since,* and *One reason for this is...*. Words and phrases that signal effect include *as a consequence, as a result, for this reason, in effect,* and *so.*

The cause may appear before or after the effect in your writing.

       effect   cause

*People's twenties are significant **because** that is when they become adults.*

       cause   effect

*Young adulthood is intense, **so** students may not experience it as positive.*

APPLY

A. Read the writing model on pages 94–96 again. With a partner, answer the following questions.

1. What words or phrases does the writer use to signal cause and effect? Circle them.

2. Does the writer show cause and effect in the same sentence? Or are causes and effects discussed in separate sentences? Underline one example of each structure.

B. With your partner, fill in the chart below with the correct causes and effects from the research proposal. Add another example you find in the proposal.

Cause	Effect
1. It may be the first time they travel abroad or get a job.	
2.	The earliest reports say that it was due to the fact that...
3. . . . because this time is filled with new and interesting experiences.	
4.	

Analyze

A. Read the research proposal on pages 94–96 again. How is the information organized? Match each subheading with its purpose below.

    a. Introduction   c. Background   e. Conclusion

    b. Literature Review   d. Methods

_b_ 1. to show that the writer is familiar with other research on the topic

___ 2. to show that the writer has the experience and knowledge to carry out the research

___ 3. to state the research purpose and give questions the research will answer

___ 4. to state the hypothesis and the larger implications of the study

___ 5. to describe the time frame and how the research is going to be done

B. With a partner, scan the writing model on pages 94–96 for words and phrases that the author uses to discuss research. Write the words and phrases you find.

current research suggests, scientists began seeing, _____

C. Read about different types of research. Then answer the questions with a partner.

> _Primary research_ collects data that does not already exist.
> **Examples:** surveys, questionnaires, interviews, observations, experiments
> _Secondary research_ looks at existing data.
> **Examples:** literature reviews, summaries, combining multiple sources of data
> _Qualitative research_ looks at people's behavior and the reasons behind it. It asks what people do and why.
> _Quantitative research_ looks for measurable or countable data. It asks how many or how often people do things.

1. Read the writing model on pages 94–96 again. Does the writer want to do primary or secondary research? How do you know?

2. Read the methods described on page 95. Is the researcher looking for qualitative or quantitative data? How do you know?

D. Discuss these questions with the class.

1. How does cause-effect writing help the writer show that she understands her research topic well?

2. What experience does the writer have that relates to the topic?

3. What explanation from the proposal do you think best explains why a significant number of memories come from the decade between ages 20 and 30?

Vocabulary Activities STEP I: Word Level

A. Use the target words and collocations in the box to complete the paragraph. Change the form and tense of the words in the box if necessary.

capable of	consent to	identical to	implicate in
insight into	interval of	persist in	

I remember it as if it were yesterday. I had just ___consented to___ allowing
                                    (1. agreed to)

the art department to use a painting of mine in its advertisement for a

university art show. I was very excited that my artwork had been chosen. I

didn't realize that I would be _____ copying another's work. After
                               (2. connected with)

the art department published my work, a student came forward and said

my painting was _____ hers. I was shocked. The paintings were
                      (3. the same as)

very similar, but I assured her I was not _____ copying another
                                   (4. able to)

student's work. I would never do that. However, she wouldn't stop telling

her story. She _____ telling the paper that I had copied her work.
               (5. continued to)

After an investigation and a brief _____ time, the school gave us
                             (6. period of)

_____ what they believed had happened. They said that we had
(7. understanding of)

both been influenced by the painting class we were taking and the painters

we were studying. The school acknowledged that our works were similar but

that I had done nothing wrong. That feeling of relief is what I remember most.

To *implicate* someone or to *implicate* someone *in* something is "to show that the person is involved in something bad, especially a crime." *Implicate* is often used in the passive voice, as the phrase *to be implicated in* something.

> The mayor <u>was **implicated** in</u> the scandal.

The noun *implication* is usually used in the plural, *implications*, and refers to "the effect that something will have on something else in the future."

> The new law will have serious **implications** for our work.

CORPUS

B. Complete each sentence with the correct form of *implicate* or *implication*.

1. The country's largest clothing store _____ *is implicated* _____ in the false advertisement scandal.

2. The state's education reform law has _____ current and future students alike.

3. The Internet company was one of several to _____ for collecting and selling information about users.

4. A group of four students _____ in a cheating scandal and forced to leave the university.

C. Complete the paragraph below with the correct forms of the target words in the box. You may use a target word more than once.

hypothesis	insight	publication	theory	thesis

Many of the articles in academic and scientific (1) _____ begin

as an idea or observation about a subject. Long before (2) _____,

researchers study the topic they are interested in. Using data and

(3) _____ into the subject, the researchers propose a

(4) _____. In some subject areas, this (5) _____ may be

used to develop a (6) _____. In others, an individual will write a

(7) _____.

Insight means "an understanding of the true nature of someone or something." The collocation *insight into* is often used.

You need __insight into__ human nature for this job.

This book gives a good __insight into__ the lives of scientists.

CORPUS

D. Match the person on the left with the subject he or she probably has insight into. Write sentences telling why each person has that insight. Use the phrase *insight into.*

___c__ 1. an expert on Abraham Lincoln

_____ 2. a parent or teacher

_____ 3. a coach or business manager

_____ 4. a psychologist

_____ 5. a person from Canada

a. insight into human behavior

b. insight into the country and its people

c. insight into his life

d. insight into how to motivate people

e. insight into child behavior

An expert on Abraham Lincoln has insight into his life because she studied him.

_____

_____

_____

_____

Vocabulary Activities STEP II: Sentence Level

E. Read the list of life events. Check (✓) the ones you think are significant milestones. Then choose two of the events. Write about why you think the events you chose are or are not significant milestones.

_____ 1. graduating from high school

_____ 2. a vacation to the beach

_____ 3. getting an iPhone

_____ 4. the first time you fly in an airplane

_____ 5. getting married

_____ 6. seeing a good movie with a friend

_____ 7. being in the hospital

Getting married is a significant milestone because then you have a life partner.

_____

_____

F. **What does the person in each job monitor? Write complete sentences. Use the word *monitor*.**

1. meteorologist *A meteorologist monitors the weather.*

2. sports writer _____

3. accountant _____

4. security guard _____

5. air traffic controller _____

G. **Rewrite the sentences numbered 1, 2, and 3 from the paragraph below. Use a target word from the box to replace each underlined word in the sentences. One word will not be used. Compare your sentences with a partner.**

hypothesis	intense	monitor	theories

Why is it that we are often not able to remember events from early childhood? Many people's first memories begin around age three.

(1) Different <u>explanations</u> have tried to answer this question. One states that we have memories from this time period, but we can't remember them.

(2) In contrast, my <u>idea</u> is that young children are overwhelmed with the world. They are using their memory to learn language and figure out the world. (3) Everything is new to young children, so everyday things, such as taking a walk, are very <u>interesting</u> experiences. In addition, because their brains are focused on language and new experiences, young children do not create memories like adults do.

1. _____

2. _____

3. _____

Grammar | Noun Clauses with *That*

A noun clause is a clause that functions as a noun in a sentence. It is a group of words that can be the sentence's subject or object. One type of noun clause begins with *that*. *That* clauses are often used in research proposals with verbs that summarize or report ideas.

main clause   noun clause
Rubin and Berntsen showed <u>*that*</u> people remember positive events in their lives.

Other verbs used to summarize or report are *suggest, demonstrate, state,* and *report.*

That clauses also follow verbs that express thoughts and opinions, such as *believe, suppose, hope, find, assume, feel,* and *think.*

main clause   noun clause
I believe <u>*that*</u> people's strongest memories are from their childhood.

Common phrases that come before *that* clauses are *due to the fact* and *the fact.*

main clause   noun clause
Strong memories may be due to the fact <u>*that*</u> events were major milestones.

That is sometimes left out when the noun clause is not the subject of the sentence.

The research suggests ~~that~~ young children process events in the same way adults do.

A. Place brackets around the *that* clause in each sentence below. Circle the subject of the clause and underline the verb.

1. Scientists have found [that the (sense of smell) <u>influences</u> memories.]

2. Studies show that the sense of smell activates memory in a stronger way than the other senses (sight, sound, and touch).

3. The fact that smell is connected to memory may have to do with the locations of the parts of the brain that process smell and memories.

4. A theory states that the other senses are not linked to the brain area where long-term memories are processed.

B. Answer the questions by completing each sentence with a *that* clause.

1. Why do you think we remember some things but not others? I feel

   that we remember things that we like and that give us a sense of who we are .

2. What theory can you use to explain why a significant number of people's memories are from their twenties? The theory I believe is

   _____.

3. What insights can you share about the factors that affect memory? One insight

   I've gained is _____.

4. What other views from friends can you share about memories? My friend

   thinks _____.

WRITING SKILL Writing a Hypothesis

LEARN

A hypothesis is an idea you have that explains something. Your idea may or may not be true, and research can show if it is true or not.

The hypothesis section of a research proposal explains what you want to prove or show, and also how you will prove or show it. Sometimes, after you do your research, your hypothesis turns out to be incorrect. That does not mean your research has failed. That is still valuable information that is worth writing about.

Follow these steps to write about your hypothesis:

1. Choose a topic and a research question about that topic. For example, you might wish to discover whether cramming (studying hard right before a test) is an effective method of studying. Your hypothesis statement might be:

   My hypothesis is that cramming is an effective way to study for quizzes or short tests, but is not effective for major exams that cover more than three weeks' worth of material.

   or

   I hypothesize that students who cram before major exams have lower scores than students who steadily reviewed material throughout the term.

2. Make sure you can test your hypothesis. Tell how you will prove it or disprove it.

   I will survey students throughout the term and then collect their final exam scores.

APPLY

Read the writing model on pages 94–96 again. Discuss these questions with a partner.

1. What statement in the research proposal tells the writer's hypothesis?

   _____

2. How will the writer test that hypothesis?

   _____

3. What results do you think the writer will find?

   _____

Collaborative Writing

A. Work with a partner. Complete these sentences. Use details from your own experiences.

1. An effective way to learn new English vocabulary is to _____

   _____.

2. A good way to study for a test is to _____

   _____.

3. One method of improving English pronunciation that really works is _____

   _____.

B. With your partner, choose one of the sentences you wrote in activity A, or use a similar idea. Create a hypothesis about the topic.

_____

C. Discuss how you would test your hypothesis. Imagine that you have one semester to do your research. Complete the chart as a guide.

Who you would study:	
Where your research would take place:	
How long your research would last:	
Materials you would need:	
What the people you are studying would do:	Steps: 1. 2. 3. 4.
How you would use your data:	
What a positive result would look like:	
What a negative result would look like:	

D. Write two paragraphs with your partner. Follow the steps below.

1. Give your hypothesis.

2. Explain how you would carry out your research.

Independent Writing

A. You are going to write a research proposal about a topic you are interested in. You do not need to do the research. You are only writing a proposal. Answer the questions below to organize your information.

1. What topic am I interested in? _____

2. What questions do I have about the topic? _____

_____

_____

3. What experience or ideas do I have that relate to the topic? _____

_____

4. What's my hypothesis? What do I expect to find out? _____

5. How will I conduct the research and collect data? For example, will I use

   interviews or journals? _____

6. What are the implications of my research? _____

B. Read about the types of research explained on page 98 again. What type of research would be best for your topic?

_____

C. Write a brief introduction to your topic. Include the information below. Complete the sentences as a guide.

1. What current research suggests:

   Current research _____.

2. What current research does not consider, which you hope to find out:

   It does not _____, however.

3. The overall purpose of your research and the topic that it relates to:

   My research will investigate _____.

4. More specific information about your research:

   My goal is to find out if _____.

D. *Hypothesis* and *theory* are often used with the same meaning in spoken English, but in research, a theory is more established than a hypothesis. Read each sentence below. Write *H* if it is a hypothesis and *T* if it is a theory.

_____ 1. Gravity holds us to the Earth.

_____ 2. The eight-year-old children will eat the sweets before the fruit if an adult isn't there to watch them.

VOCABULARY TIP

A hypothesis is an idea or explanation of something that is based on a few known facts but has not been proven to be true yet.

A theory is a well-established idea that has been developed from repeated observations and tests.

E. Using the type of research you chose in activity B, plan your research method. Complete the chart below as a guide.

Number of people involved:	
How you will gather data:	
Time frame of research:	
How you will evaluate data:	

F. Establish yourself as being able to do the research. What experiences and interests do you have that are related to the subject? Write them below.

_____

_____

_____

G. Plan your conclusion. Complete the sentences below as a guide.

1. (state what you expect the results of your research to be) My hypothesis is

   that _____

   _____.

2. (state what your results will prove) If my hypothesis is correct, the

   implications are _____

   _____.

H. Write your research proposal. Use the questions you answered in activity A and the sentences you wrote in activities C through G. Follow the format of the writing model on pages 94–96 without the literature review. Use target vocabulary from page 93.

REVISE AND EDIT

A. Read your research proposal. Answer the questions below, and make revisions to your proposal as needed.

1. Check (✓) the information you included in your research proposal.

   ☐ introduction

   ☐ background and methodology

   ☐ research implications

   ☐ hypothesis and conclusion

   ☐ subheadings to show text structure

   ☐ conclusion

2. Look at the information you did not include. Would adding that information improve your research proposal?

Grammar for Editing | Indirect Speech

Indirect speech states someone else's ideas without quoting the exact words that person said. When you use indirect speech, introduce the idea with a *that* clause.

> Other researchers (Leist et al., 2010) suggest *that* the brain stores events that define who we are.

Although you are not quoting someone else directly, indirect speech is still reporting someone else's idea. Credit the source of your information. The example above uses parentheses to list the author and year of publication.

B. Check the language in your research proposal. Revise and edit as needed.

Language Checklist
☐ I used target words in my research proposal.
☐ I used words and phrases that signal causes and effects.
☐ I used *that* clauses to summarize and report ideas.
☐ I introduced indirect speech correctly.

C. Check your research proposal again. Repeat activities A and B.

Self-Assessment Review: Go back to page 93 and reassess your knowledge of the target vocabulary. How has your understanding of the words changed? What words do you feel most comfortable using now?

UNIT 8

Finding a Formula for Motivation

In this unit, you will

> analyze a magazine article and learn how it is used in psychology.
> use compare-contrast writing.
> increase your understanding of the target academic words for this unit.

WRITING SKILLS

> Examples
> Comparing and Contrasting
> **GRAMMAR** Words and Phrases of Contrast and Concession

Self-Assessment

Think about how well you know each target word, and check (✓) the appropriate column. I have…

TARGET WORDS	never seen the word before.	heard or seen the word but am not sure what it means.	heard or seen the word and understand what it means.	used the word confidently in *either* speaking or writing.
AWL				
clarify				
conform				
contrary				
differentiate				
ethic				
🔑 formula				
🔑 impose				
parameter				
passive				
precede				
🔑 principle				
rational				
successor				
🔑 valid				

🔑 Oxford 3000™ keywords

Building Knowledge

Read these questions. Discuss your answers in a small group.

1. What magazines do you read?

2. Why do you think magazines are so popular?

3. Why do you think people do dangerous things?

Writing Model

A magazine article often summarizes the similarities and differences among theories on a particular topic. Read about different theories of motivation.

Can We Truly Answer *Why*?

BY SAHEED BATSWAN

What motivates[1] a man to string a wire 300 feet off the ground and walk across it? A mistake could cost him his life. Yet, Philippe Petit decided to walk across a wire between
5 two towers of the Sydney Harbor Bridge as the water flowed below. How do we **rationalize** his behavior? Motivation. It's something we have but don't fully understand. Was it his own will[2] that motivated him, or was it the appreciation of gathering crowds that
10 kept him going?

There are many theories to define a set of **parameters** of human motivation. One theory involves *intrinsic* and *extrinsic* motivation. People who are intrinsically motivated are also internally
15 motivated. They do something simply because they want to. They might want to express themselves or have a desire to learn. On the **contrary**, extrinsic motivation is external motivation. It might be because someone seeks approval, status, or recognition. To **differentiate** between these two types of motivation, use yourself as an example. If you weren't being graded on a test, would you still study for
20 it? Perhaps you would, but maybe not all night. It's the intrinsic motivation that makes you want to do well on the test. You want to **validate** your sense of self. You prove to yourself that you can learn the material and you are smart. It's the extrinsic motivation that makes you try for the grade, or the approval of the instructor. Both **principles** come from a *cognitive theory* of motivation. Cognitive

Some people choose a city structure as a place for risky behavior.

---

[1] *motivate:* to make someone want to do something
[2] *will:* the power of your mind that makes you do something

theories say that our behavior is caused by how we think about information.

The cognitive theory, though, raises the question of **ethics**. It says that if people receive rewards for something that they are already intrinsically motivated to do, they will *lose* motivation. Again, go back to the example of grades. The idea is that if you were motivated to do well in school without the need for a grade, then you would learn simply because you desire to learn. However, once grades were **imposed**, you would no longer want to learn. Your intrinsic motivation would weaken, and you would no longer do as well. In fact, an article in

What motivates students to do well on tests?

the magazine *Psychology Today* explains that managers could use the cognitive theory to pay workers less, or not at all! That would be illegal and **unethical**, of course. The thinking is that if managers paid workers for what they already like to do, workers would do less work.

There hasn't been a **successor** to the cognitive theory. It is still the most popular theory for motivation out there. However, a second theory is the *self-determination theory*. The self-determination theory differs from the cognitive theory because it allows for a combination of both intrinsic and extrinsic motivation. You may be motivated by both your own desire to do well and approval from others. The self-determination theory **clarifies** some other aspects of motivation. One key element is autonomy, or the ability to control one's self. The basic idea is that people like to feel they are in control, and not just **conforming** to expectations placed on them. They want to express themselves. They are actively, not **passively**, involved in making decisions about their life.

These two theories to explain motivation are not the only ones that exist. Theories that **preceded** these tended to focus on humans' drive[3] to get their needs met. Two of these theories argued opposite views. The first, *drive reduction theory*, stated that most people just want stability. They desire to be satisfied. Conversely, the *arousal* or *excitement theory* suggests that humans want the opposite of stability. They want excitement. They are always looking to take things to the next level.[4] The image of Philippe Petit on top of a thin wire hundreds of feet in the air comes to mind. However, this theory doesn't just apply to the extreme risk taker. It claims that everyone finds his or her own level of excitement. So, for example, if walking across a wire sounds too dangerous, you might find excitement in mountain biking.

Humans are complex. Determining why they do what they do isn't a simple **formula**. Each theory offers its own insight into human behavior. Yet, nothing is certain. As long as there are scientists to study us, there will also be people who challenge expectations, walking a fine line between this theory and the next.

---

[3] *drive:* the energy and determination you need to succeed in doing something
[4] *take things to the next level:* challenge the limits, go on to something more difficult

LEARN

When you write about an abstract theory, give an example to make it concrete and easy to understand. Continuing an example throughout an article can also make the article interesting.

Mark examples with the signal phrases *such as*, *One example of*, *For example*, or *For instance*:

> Some students study for intrinsic reasons **such as** feeling they did a good job.

> **One example of** intrinsic motivation is personal pride in a job well done.

> However, teachers grade tests because they know extrinsic motivation works.
> **For example / For instance**, no one wants a failing grade.

APPLY

Read the article on pages 110–111 again. Underline the examples. Answer the questions below with a partner.

1. The article begins with an example. What is the purpose of that example?

   a. to explain what the word "motivation" means

   b. to make readers interested in what motivates some people

   c. to show readers what types of motivation will be explained in the article

2. In what other paragraph does that example appear? Why does the author mention it again?

3. What is the purpose of the example in the second paragraph?

4. Does that example help you understand the ideas? Why, or why not?

Analyze

A. Read the article on pages 110–111 again. Complete the outline below with a partner.

  I. Theories of _____Motivation_____

    A. Cognitive Theory

      1. Intrinsic motivation versus _____ motivation

        a. _____ motivation is motivation that comes from within.

          An example is _____.

        b. Extrinsic motivation is _____.

          An example is _____.

      2. Conclusion: An extrinsic reward weakens _____.

B. _____

    1. Is not the _____ to cognitive theory

    2. Allows for _____

    3. One key element is _____.

C. Theories that focus on humans' _____

    1. _____ theory versus the excitement theory

       a. According to drive reduction theory, people want _____.

       b. According to the excitement theory, people want _____.

B. Answer the questions below with a partner. Use the outline you made in activity A.

1. Which paragraph(s) are about only one theory?

2. Which paragraph is about more than one theory?

3. Look at the second and fifth paragraphs. What does the author compare and contrast in each?

   a. Paragraph 2: _____

   b. Paragraph 5: _____

4. Why do you think the author put the *drive reduction theory* and *excitement theory* together in one paragraph?

5. In the fourth paragraph, what does the author compare to the self-determination theory?

6. The third paragraph is about the cognitive theory. Why do you think it doesn't contain comparisons or examples?

C. Discuss the questions below as a class.

1. Which theory of motivation do you think best explains human behavior? Why?

2. What examples from your own experience or knowledge support your opinion?

A. Read this excerpt from a lecture about human motivation. Circle the word or phrase in parentheses that has the same meaning as the underlined word in each sentence. Compare your answers with a partner.

Understanding what motivates people to do things should be easy, right? Human beings are <u>rational</u> (1. ethical, (reasonable,) smart). They <u>conform to</u> (2. create, follow, need) basic <u>principles</u> (3. goals, leaders, standards) of behavior. Raise your hand if you agree with what I just said. Ah, if you did not raise your hand you are correct. <u>On the contrary</u> (4. In addition to, In contrast, Similarly) to what I said at the start of the lecture, human motivation is a complex subject. There is no simple <u>formula</u> (5. answer, result, rule) you can memorize that sets the <u>parameters</u> (6. limits, obligations, traditions) for human motivation. Think how easy this psychology course would be if all you had to do was learn a formula! Instead, in this course we will study why it is not possible to <u>impose</u> (7. put, take, teach) one theory of motivation on all people. You will learn why it is important to <u>differentiate</u> (8. see conclusions, see differences, see opposites) between types of motivation. In today's lecture I will present and try to <u>clarify</u> (9. discuss, enlarge, make clear) the difference between *intrinsic* and *extrinsic* motivation. These are two <u>valid</u> (10. accepted, confused, unrelated) theories in the study of human motivation.

B. Complete the Word Form chart with forms of the word *differentiate* and *ethics*.

Word Form Chart			
Noun	**Verb**	**Adjective**	**Adverb**
	differentiate		_____
ethics	_____	unethical	

C. Read each behavior below. Write *E* if it is ethical or *U* if it is unethical. Discuss your answers with a partner.

_E_ respecting others

___ downloading music illegally

___ taking credit for something you didn't do

___ keeping a promise to a friend

___ doing research online

___ borrowing something and not returning it

___ helping a classmate who doesn't understand something

___ asking someone if you can copy their homework

___ discrimination

D. Complete each sentence with the correct form of *differentiate* from the chart in activity B.

1. Some sea animals have difficulty __differentiating__ between jellyfish, a food source, and plastic bags, which are harmful to them.

2. _____ refers to taking a whole and dividing it into many parts.

3. Many laws _____ people into three age groups: under 18, 18–65, and over 65.

4. You might need glasses if you cannot _____ faces from a distance.

5. The colleges were _____ by how many students they had.

Passive is an adjective that means "showing no reaction, feeling, or interest." The opposite is *active*.

*Television encourages people to be **passive**.*

CORPUS

E. Read the behaviors. Write whether each one is active or passive. Share your reasons with a partner.

_____active_____ 1. taking a walk

_____ 2. eating breakfast

_____ 3. reading a book

_____ 4. talking on the phone

_____ 5. listening to a lecture

Valid refers to something that is "logical or true." The opposite is *invalid*.

> *When arguing against a parking ticket, she made the **valid** point that there was no sign showing the parking regulations.*

Valid commonly occurs with certain nouns including *theory, finding, result, conclusion, argument, point, reason, criticism,* and *assumption*.

CORPUS

F. Read the main points and examples below. Cross out the example that isn't valid. Discuss your choice with a partner, using one of the collocations from above.

1. Offering rewards to students for getting good grades does more harm than good.

   a. For example, once students are given rewards, they lose motivation to learn unless there is an external reward offered.

   b. For instance, my son has increased the number of books he reads since his school began offering free use of iPads for students who read ten books a month.

2. We have become too dependent on technology. As a result, we are losing our ability to memorize information. We use technology to tell us when to eat, sleep, and study.

   a. On the contrary, I would argue that technology allows us to better remember important information and let our smartphones remember the details of meeting times and places.

   b. Just yesterday, I forgot to go to a meeting at my son's school. I hadn't put it into my smartphone, and I certainly didn't recall it on my own until the school called.

G. Write a sentence about four events in the time line. In each sentence, use the target words *successor* or *precede*.

Timeline of Events

| Garcia is elected governor | Garcia makes unpopular decisions | Garcia loses the next election to Kim | Kim is popular with voters, serves two terms | Kim takes a job with federal government, replacing Marshall | Koury wins election for governor, serves one term |

1. _____

2. _____

3. _____

4. _____

H. Read each scenario. Answer the question using a form of *impose* or *conform*.

1. "I'm sorry," Jenny said to her manager. "I know you are leaving, but could you sign my request for vacation time?"

   Who imposed on whom? *Jenny imposed on her manager.* _____

2. "If you want to continue working here, you will have to follow our dress code policy," said Mikail to Ibrihim.

   Who needs to conform to what? _____

3. "The law charges any business a fine if it does not offer its employees paid holidays," explained Aliaa.

   What is being imposed on what? _____

I. Rewrite each sentence using the correct form of a target word in the box.

| clarify | differentiate | parameters | passive | rational |

1. The university needs rules about students' use of laptops during lectures.

   The university should set parameters for when students can use laptops in class.

2. Students must be active, not uninvolved, participants in their education.

   _____

3. I want to make this easier for you to understand. Attendance is mandatory.

   _____

4. The school has a logical argument for not giving students grades.

   _____

Grammar | Words and Phrases of Contrast and Concession

A contrast shows the differences between two things. Use *but, however, in contrast,* and *conversely* to show how two things differ.

But is a conjunction and connects two clauses with a comma.

> There are many theories on motivation, <u>but</u> only a couple are well-known.

However, in contrast, and *conversely* are adverbs that can be used in the beginning of a sentence followed by a comma.

> I think that the self-determination theory best explains human motivation. <u>However</u>, my best friend believes in the arousal theory. She thinks we need constant excitement.

To concede is to admit an argument may be true but then argue a contrasting point. Use *yet, even though,* or *although* to show concessions.

Yet is a conjunction and connects two clauses with a comma.

> Each theory offers its own insight into human behavior, <u>yet</u> neither is certain.

Even though and *although* begin dependent clauses that must be in the same sentence as an independent clause.

> <u>Even though I understand the points made by the writer about motivation</u>, I don't think any of the theories clearly show the complexity of human motivation.

A. Read the passage below. Circle the words that signal contrast. Then answer the questions.

Researchers wanted to see if offering a reward would improve young children's test scores. First, all the children took the test. Then seven weeks later, the students were given the same test. This time, however, some students were given candy for each answer they got correct. The researchers compared the first test scores to the second test. The test scores of the students in the group that received the candy significantly improved. Although there was improvement, new research shows that the first test results may be a better predictor of children's future achievement. The idea is that even though students were able to improve their test scores, what matters is how well they perform without a reward. It turns out that in life, those that are motivated from within often achieve more.

1. What is the contrast, or difference, the second time the students take the test?

   _____

2. What word concedes that candy improved students' scores? _____

3. What is the point the writer argues after this concession? _____

4. What word or phrase signals the writer's second concession? _____

5. What does the writer go on to argue? _____

B. Read each statement. Rewrite the information using a signal word to show the contrast or concession that is being made. Compare your answers with a partner.

1. I really enjoy my job. It's nice to get paid. I think I would do it for free.

   I really enjoy my job. It's nice to get paid, yet I think I would do it for free.

   _____

2. My son's school allows him to choose what he wants to learn. The idea is that he will become self-motivated. I agree with the theory in principle. I think he could use a little guidance and help in his learning.

   _____

   _____

3. Several school systems have tried to offer rewards for students to perform better. The programs didn't achieve the results administrators were looking for.

   _____

   _____

4. One program offered money to teachers whose students' test scores improved. The program was very expensive and did not affect students' performance.

   _____

   _____

C. Should teachers be given rewards to motivate children to perform better? Write a statement that shows a contrast or concession to sum up your thoughts.

   _____

   _____

LEARN

A comparison shows how two things are similar. A contrast shows the differences. You can compare two things that seem different (to show unexpected similarities), and contrast two things that seem similar (to highlight their differences).

Consider these questions to understand the relationship between your main ideas:

- What do they have in common?

- How does each idea differ?

- Do the similarities mean anything? For example, that the ideas are equally important?

- Do the differences mean anything? For example, that one idea is superior in some way to another?

Use these words and phrases to write about comparisons and contrasts:

Comparison	Contrast
Both ... and ...	In contrast,
Similarly,	Unlike
Likewise,	On the contrary,
In the same way,	On the other hand,
too / also / and	however / but / yet

APPLY

A. Complete the sentences with expressions for comparing or contrasting.

1. _____ intrinsic _____ extrinsic motivation attempt to explain human behavior.

2. _____ extrinsically motivated students, intrinsically motivated ones work to prove something to themselves.

3. An intrinsically motivated student might not be interested in grades. _____, an externally motivated student appreciates this evaluation.

4. The label of intrinsic motivation grew out of cognitive theory. _____, this theory gave rise to the term *extrinsic motivation*.

B. Read the article on pages 110–111 again. Underline three expressions of comparison or contrast. Then share your expressions with a partner. Did you find the same ones or different ones?

C. Use the writing model on pages 110–111 to complete the chart below. Note whether the features are similar or different.

Intrinsic	Extrinsic	Similar or different?
A type of motivation	_A type of motivation_	_similar_
People are internally motivated.	People are externally motivated.	_different_
Example: Students work _____.	Example: Students work to gain approval or recognition.	_____
Example: A student studies for a test because he or she wants to validate a sense of self.	Example: A student studies for a test _____.	_____
Comes from cognitive theory of motivation	_____.	_____

Collaborative Writing

A. With a partner, use the chart above to answer the questions about intrinsic and extrinsic motivation.

1. What is intrinsic motivation? _____

   _____

2. Give your own example of intrinsic motivation. _____

   _____

3. What is extrinsic motivation? _____

   _____

4. Give your own example of extrinsic motivation. _____

   _____

5. How are the two theories alike? _____

   _____

6. How are they different? _____

   _____

B. Use your answers from activity A to write sentences that compare and contrast the two types of motivation. Complete the sentences below as a guide.

Both intrinsic and extrinsic motivation _____.

Extrinsic motivation _____. Similarly, intrinsic

motivation _____.

Unlike extrinsic motivation, intrinsic motivation _____.

Intrinsic motivation _____. On the other

hand, extrinsic motivation _____.

C. With your partner, decide how you will organize two or three brief paragraphs. Pick the organization method you prefer from the list below and explain your choice.

- one paragraph comparing the two types of motivation, one paragraph contrasting the two types of motivation

- one paragraph focusing on one type of motivation, one paragraph focusing on what makes the other type different, and a third paragraph on what makes them similar

- one paragraph focusing on one type of motivation, one paragraph focusing on what makes the other type similar, and a third paragraph on what makes them different

- another type of organization: _____

  Reasons for your choice: _____

D. Write two paragraphs that compare and contrast internal and external motivation. Use your examples from activity A and sentences from activity B.

E. Share your paragraphs with the class. As a class, discuss these questions.

1. Did the examples provided help you understand the principles?

2. Did the paragraphs make you feel that intrinsic and extrinsic motivation are very different, very similar, or neither? What do you think was the writers' goal?

3. What did different groups do differently from each other? How did that make the paragraphs easier or more difficult to understand?

Independent Writing

A. You will write an article comparing and contrasting positive and negative reinforcement. Think of a task that you need motivation to complete. For example, studying for tests, learning a new skill, or doing a chore. Write your task below.

Task that requires motivation: _____

B. What motivates you to complete that task? Complete the chart below with your previous experiences of positive and negative reinforcement. For example, a teacher giving you points for doing your homework is positive reinforcement, and a teacher subtracting points from your grade for not doing your homework is negative reinforcement.

Positive reinforcements	Negative reinforcements
•	•
•	•
•	•
•	•

C. Plan your body paragraphs. Write a topic sentence for each paragraph explaining the type of reinforcement and how well it worked.

_____

_____

_____

D. Plan your introduction and conclusion paragraphs. Answer the questions below as a guide.

1. How can you introduce the topic? Is there a question that will engage your reader? Is there an example that will clearly illustrate the idea?

_____

2. How can you conclude your article? Can you answer the question from the introduction or return to an example you used? Can you draw conclusions about how reinforcements motivate you?

_____

E. Write an article that compares and contrasts these two types of reinforcement and explain what works best for you. Use your notes from activities B, C, and D to develop your paragraphs. Use target vocabulary words from page 109, examples to support your points, and signal words of comparison or contrast to help your reader see the relationships between your ideas.

A. Read your magazine article. Answer the questions below, and make revisions to your article as needed.

1. Check (✓) the information you included in your magazine article.

   ☐ an example or question to engage the reader

   ☐ supporting examples

   ☐ definitions of abstract ideas

   ☐ words and phrases of comparison and contrast

   ☐ a conclusion that answers a question or sums up the issue

2. Look at the information you did not include. Would adding that information make your article more informative and appealing?

Grammar for Editing | Using Transitions and Subordinators

If a transition word or phrase is at the beginning of a sentence, follow it with a comma. If it combines two independent clauses into a single sentence, precede it with a semicolon as well.

I don't believe in giving teachers financial rewards to improve test scores_. In contrast,_ my best friend who is a teacher thinks that teachers and students benefit from rewards.

In principle, rewards sound like a good way to increase student interest_; however,_ over time rewards may not be the best way to motivate.

Place a comma before the conjunction *but* to link two independent clauses.

Children may be motivated by rewards_, but_ I think motivation is largely determined by personality.

B. Check the language in your article. Revise and edit as needed.

Language Checklist
☐ I used target words in my article.
☐ I used signal words to show relationships.
☐ I used words and phrases of contrast and concession.
☐ I used correct punctuation when showing relationships.

C. Check your magazine article again. Repeat activities A and B.

Self-Assessment Review: Go back to page 109 and reassess your knowledge of the target vocabulary. How has your understanding of the words changed? What words do you feel most comfortable using now?

UNIT 9

Designing a Philosophy

In this unit, you will

> analyze a case study and learn how it is used in business.
> use personal narrative writing.
> increase your understanding of the target academic words for this unit.

WRITING SKILLS

> Personal Narrative
> Sentence Variety
> **GRAMMAR** Sentence Structure

Self-Assessment

Think about how well you know each target word, and check (✓) the appropriate column. I have...

TARGET WORDS	never seen the word before.	heard or seen the word but am not sure what it means.	heard or seen the word and understand what it means.	used the word confidently in *either* speaking or writing.
AWL				
assign				
🔑 assure				
🔑 classic				
🔑 concept				
🔑 considerable				
🔑 element				
🔑 export				
🔑 invest				
minimize				
🔑 philosophy				
🔑 precise				
🔑 register				
revenue				
🔑 ultimate				

🔑 Oxford 3000™ keywords

Building Knowledge

Read these questions. Discuss your answers in a small group.

1. What are some logos you know well? Talk about their shape, design, and meaning.

2. Where do you usually see logos displayed?

3. What are some factors a business should take into consideration when designing a logo?

Writing Model

A case study is the detailed story of the development of a product or situation. Read a case study about how a designer created a logo for a digital and print publisher.

Designing a Wayzgoose

The first question I asked the small independent publisher Wayzgoose Press, when I was **assigned** to design a website and a logo for them, was what
5 **precisely** a "wayzgoose" was. Some sort of bird? I had no idea. I could have checked a dictionary, but I wanted to hear it in their own words to help me understand their **philosophy**. A wayzgoose, they explained, was an old
10 British custom for publishers. Back before the use of electric lights, printing houses had a special celebration each fall that marked the time when printers had to start working by candlelight because the sun was setting earlier.
15 The printing establishment would take a trip into the country and have a large picnic for all of the print workers.

A soaring goose: the inspiration for the logo

My challenge was to find the strength in the word *wayzgoose* and use that to create a visually
20 appealing logo. The design had to be familiar as well as entice[1] the viewer to seek the whole story. And it had to meet the publisher's goals: to clearly identify their brand, tell their story, and help them bring in **revenue**.

COMMUNICATING WITH COLOR AND FONT

25 Colors play a very important part in design. Color is a form of nonverbal communication with **considerable** power, and different individuals have different preferences. After a few emails and phone calls with Wayzgoose
30 Press, I discovered that the client liked the warm rich tones of hot desert sands. Those are also colors that show up well on different website browsers. **Ultimately**, a website needs to be readable on a great number of different devices.
35 I showed the senior editor some sample color palettes,[2] and once she **assured** me that she liked the reds and golds, I was ready to design the logo.

Typography[3] was crucial.[4] The word
40 *wayzgoose* had to look familiar and understandable at a glance. But it also had to make the viewer take a second look. I wanted the *w* to be the main **element** of the logo. I experimented with a **considerable** number of
45 typefaces during this process. I selected the font Arabic Typesetting because I liked its clean, **classic** look.

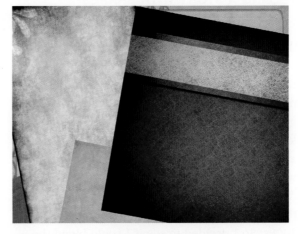

Colors are part of a company's message.

Font can be as important as the words themselves.

WAYZGOOSE PRESS

The final type treatment

---

[1] *entice:* to persuade someone to go somewhere or do something, usually by offering them something
[2] *palette:* a range of colors
[3] *typography:* the style and appearance of printed letters
[4] *crucial:* extremely important because it will affect other things

TELLING A STORY WITH SHAPES

Somehow, though, the logo still didn't tell the whole story. I needed the *w* to have
50 something like motion or flight. I **invested** some time in just drawing whatever came into my mind. I decided that I wanted the *w* to fly like a goose. A wayzgoose is not a type of animal, I know, but I felt that customers would
55 automatically think of a big, long-necked goose when they encountered the word—just as I had. And, in fact, it's possible that goose was eaten at the original wayzgoose picnics back in the 1800s. So I decided to see if I could blend the
60 **concept** of a goose with the *w*.

A goose needs a neck, so if the *w* was also the goose, then the goose would be flying into the ground—not the image I wanted to present! I wanted this goose to soar. The goose therefore
65 needed to become a separate **element** and not the main *w*. I **minimized** the tail, enlarged the wings, tipped[5] the goose up to fly—and I had it. Once a tag line[6] was added and colors were chosen, we had an identity for Wayzgoose Press.

THE FINISHED LOGO

70 The mark of a good logo design is flexibility. The design can be used complete or in part for a variety of formats. The client needed to easily **export** the design to print media while maintaining consistency. One aspect of the logo
75 that the publisher particularly appreciated was that the goose logo, positioned vertically, looked like a bird in flight; however, on the spine of a book, when the book was laid horizontally, it easily **registered** as a *w*.

80 And thus, a logo was born.
—DJ Rogers, DJ Rogers Design

---

[5] *tipped:* moved so that one end is higher than the other
[6] *tag line:* a phrase used in an advertisement that is important and easy to remember

Different drawings of the letter W

The finished Wayzgoose logo

LEARN

A case study is a detailed explanation of how or why something developed. Case studies are examples of *personal narratives*—they tell about one person's experience and offer insight into what the writer was thinking at different stages of a project's development.

You may have learned not to use the first person pronouns *I* or *we* in formal writing in order to be professional rather than personal. But in case studies, the first person is appropriate.

Use *I* or *we* for these purposes in your personal narrative:

- to explain steps you took to achieve a result

- to explain a change in how you viewed or thought about something

- to discuss a problem or difficulty, and how you overcame it

APPLY

A. Read the case study on pages 126–128 again. Underline the sentences where the writer uses first person pronouns. About what percent of the writing model are they?

B. Read the fifth and sixth paragraphs of the case study again. Write about how that personal narrative helps you understand the development of the logo. Share your answer with a partner.

_____

_____

C. Personal narrative writing explains the writer's thought process and decisions. Write *PN* by the ideas below that would likely be written using personal narrative. Discuss your answers with a partner.

____ 1. a description of a wayzgoose event in the 1800s

____ 2. why Arabic Typesetting is considered a classic-looking font

____ 3. how the designer was chosen for this job

____ 4. the designer's impression of the publisher's existing website

____ 5. a description of the types of books Wayzgoose Press publishes

____ 6. how the designer tried a symbol of a goose and why she changed her mind

____ 7. a profile of typical customers of Wayzgoose Press

____ 8. why the designer feels that simple designs are more effective than complex ones

Analyze

A. Read the case study on pages 126–128 again. How is it organized? Number the sections in the order they appear.

_____ combining the letter *w* with the concept of a goose

_____ comment on the overall effectiveness of the design

__1__ meaning of the publisher's name

_____ separating the logo from the word

_____ the use of color

_____ the use of typography

_____ what the designer wanted the logo to show

B. Which sections of the case study on pages 126–128 contain personal narrative? Write *PN* next to each of those sections in activity A.

C. Read the last paragraph of the writing model. It does not use personal narrative. Answer the questions below with a partner.

1. What are the first three sentences of the paragraph about?

2. Why do you think the writer chose not to use personal narrative for part of the last paragraph?

D. Discuss these questions with a partner.

1. Who do you think is the audience for this type of writing?

2. The pictures show the logo design clearly. Why does the designer also tell her story and describe the logo in words?

3. What is the purpose of a case study? Why might a story of how something was developed be important?

Vocabulary Activities STEP I: Word Level

A. Three target words contain a double consonant and have two syllables. Record the words below. Draw a line to separate each word into two syllables.

1. _____ as|sign _____

2. _____

3. _____

B. Match each target word to the list of words that it collocates with. Use a dictionary and the writing model on pages 126–128 for clues. Some lists will collocate with more than one target word.

considerable	export	invest	minimize	~~revenue~~

1. expected, tax, target, more, additional _____*revenue*_____

2. _____ time, money, energy, resources, labor

3. _____ risk, use, stress, differences, damage

4. _____ effort, value, damage, energy, interest

5. _____ goods, services, products, oil, tax

When used as a verb, *register* can be transitive (followed by an object) or intransitive (without an object). *Register* has several meanings.

1. to put a name or other information on a formal list

    *I **registered** for an English class.* (intransitive)

2. to show an amount on a measuring instrument

    *The thermostat in our house **registered** 55 degrees Fahrenheit.* (transitive)

3. to show feelings or opinions

    *The principal's face **registered** disapproval as he scolded the children for their behavior.* (transitive)

CORPUS

C. What do all three definitions of *register* have in common? How are their meanings related? Write your ideas below. Then discuss your answer with a partner.

_____

_____

D. Read each sentence. Record the number of the definition above that best matches the use of *register* in each sentence. If *register* is used transitively, underline the object.

_1_ 1. I didn't get into the class I wanted to take because I didn't register in time.

___ 2. Her face registered surprise when I showed up at the hospital to see her.

___ 3. My car wouldn't start. I looked at the gas gauge. It registered empty.

___ 4. To register for the conference, you need a valid driver's license.

Philosophy refers to "a belief or set of beliefs that tries to explain the meaning of life or give rules about how to behave." In this sense, it is countable.

The company Apple embraces several philosophies, each focused on the customers' needs.

The noun *philosophy* can also refer to "the study of beliefs about the meaning of life." In this sense, it is uncountable.

My brother is studying philosophy. He is learning about Aristotle.

 CORPUS

E. Read each sentence. Is *philosophy* countable or uncountable? Write *U* if it is uncountable or *C* if it is countable.

___U__ 1. The role of philosophy has always been to make us question our beliefs.

_____ 2. As a manager, my philosophy is that you have to know your employees and understand their everyday work in order to improve practices.

_____ 3. Their products and business philosophies are similar.

_____ 4. One philosophy I agree with is that education must allow students to choose how they learn best.

_____ 5. In addition to literature, my sister teaches philosophy at the college level.

Vocabulary Activities STEP II: Sentence Level

An *element* is "one part of something." Common adjectives used before element are *key, essential, necessary, basic, important,* and *main*.

The most important element of my job decision was location.

The idioms *in your element* and *out of your element* refer to how comfortable you are in a situation.

Once we transferred our daughter to a new school, she was <u>in her element</u> and much happier.

 CORPUS

F. Write sentences about the ideas below. Use a collocation or idiom from the corpus box above in each sentence.

1. elements of a healthy diet *Some key elements of a healthy diet are fruits and* _____

   vegetables. _____

2. elements of happiness _____

3. elements of a good relationship _____

4. in my element _____

5. out of my element _____

G. Read about a successful marketing campaign. Rewrite the sentences using the target words from the box. Compare your summary to a partner's.

concept	philosophy	precise	revenue	ultimate

The idea behind Procter & Gamble's million-dollar Olympic marketing campaign was straightforward. Show children as young athletes—their joys and defeats. Then show their proud mothers. Procter & Gamble generated income in countries all over the world from the "Thank You, Mom" video ad. It was their greatest marketing achievement. All their different products were connected under one belief that recognized the families behind the athletes. While the company doesn't release the exact amount it spent on financing the campaign, the success shows it paid off.

_____

_____

_____

_____

_____

As a verb, *assure* means "to tell someone something confidently so that the person doesn't doubt it any more." *Assurance*, the noun form, is often used with *give* or *offer* and refers to "a statement of guarantee."

> I **assured** her that the logo design would be finished on schedule.

> They gave me **assurance** that their firm's logo would be different from mine.

The adjective form, *assured*, means that something is certain to happen.

> With so little time left in the game, our team's victory was **assured**.

CORPUS

H. Read each statement below. How would you reply to someone who said it to you? Use a form of *assure* in your answer. Share your answers with a partner.

1. "I've been practicing driving for months. I hope I pass the driving test."

   Because you practiced, passing the test is assured.

2. "This is my first winter in a cold country. I'm really worried about the snow."

   _____

3. "Will your logo design really help me bring in more revenue?"

   _____

4. "I made all the arrangements for the celebration weeks ahead of time."

   _____

Grammar | Sentence Structure

Using a variety of sentence types can make your writing more interesting. It can also help emphasize important points and show relationships between ideas.

A complex sentence contains a dependent and an independent clause. Each type of clause has a subject and a verb. An independent clause can form a sentence by itself, but a dependent clause cannot stand on its own.

The dependent clause often describes or gives more information about the independent clause.

dependent clause   independent clause
Before the use of electric lights, printing houses had a special celebration each fall.

However, the writing model does not consist entirely of complex sentences. The writer uses short, declarative sentences to emphasize important ideas.

independent clause
Typography was crucial.

The simple sentence, which contains one independent clause, is powerful because it is short. The sentence interrupts the audience's speed of reading, so the audience notices it.

Writers use compound sentences to show relationships between ideas. Compound sentences contain two independent clauses. The coordinating conjunction *and* connects two independent clauses. *But* contrasts them.

independent clause   independent clause
I could have checked a dictionary, *but* I wanted to hear it in their own words to help me understand their philosophy.

A. Put brackets ([ ]) around each clause in the sentences below. Then label each sentence *complex, compound,* or *simple.*

_____simple_____ 1. [A logo is more than an image].

_____ 2. If it is done well, it expresses a philosophy.

_____ 3. The logo must represent the creativity and expertise that the school encourages.

_____ 4. This simple image states the purpose of the organization, and it communicates that purpose visually.

_____ 5. The company saw several logo designs before choosing one.

B. Rewrite the passage below to include more sentence variety and better emphasize the relationships between ideas.

Apple doesn't sell apples. Apple sells computers. Apple sells technology. Why is the logo an apple? In fact, the Apple logo has redefined the word *apple*. In certain conversations and environments, the word or image of an apple is more strongly associated with the company than with the fruit. The symbol is recognized all over the world. Perhaps that is the key to its success. The business used a concrete image. They used a familiar shape. The shape had global recognition. It was simple in its form. The word *apple* is part of many people's vocabularies. It is one word. It is one image. It can't go out of date. It cannot become part of the past. It's an apple.

_____

_____

_____

_____

_____

_____

_____

_____

_____

_____

_____

_____

_____

C. Read the case study on pages 126–128 again. Answer the questions below with a partner.

1. Are there any other short, simple sentences in the writing model similar to "Typography was crucial."? Write two examples here:

_____

_____

2. Why do you think the writer chose to present those ideas by themselves in short sentences?

3. Are there any compound or complex sentences in the writing model that you would rewrite as two separate sentences? Why would you do so?

WRITING SKILL · Sentence Variety

LEARN

Your writing is more interesting and easier to read when you use a variety of sentences: simple, compound, and complex; short and long; statements and questions.

Check for sentence variety after you have written a draft of your text. Ask yourself these questions when you assess your writing:

- How many (what percent) of my sentences are in the *subject + verb + object* pattern? How many are in other patterns?

  subject + verb + object: *I designed the logo on my laptop.*
  subject + verb + indirect object + direct object: *I showed him my new design.*

- Can I move some phrases or expressions to different parts of the sentence?

  I sketched a rough draft in my notebook.
  In my notebook, I sketched a rough draft.

- Are all of my sentences about the same length?

- Can any be combined into longer sentences?

- Are there places where I could use a short sentence or a fragment for special emphasis?

- Can I use a question to get my readers' attention?

- Can I use a series of three or more elements, separated by commas?

  This logo is simple, attractive, and familiar.

APPLY

A. Read the case study on pages 126–128 again. Underline an example of each of these elements.

1. a short sentence

2. a question

3. a simple sentence

4. a sentence that begins with a dependent clause

5. a sentence with two different connectors (such as *and, so, but, then, or, because,* etc.)

B. Work with a partner. Share the sentences that you underlined in activity A. Then discuss the structure of the sentences that appear before and after each sentence that you underlined.

Collaborative Writing

A. Read about this company.

Green Travel is a new travel agency dedicated to environmentally responsible tourism. We run a variety of group eco-tours and help solo travelers plan trips that don't negatively impact our beautiful planet. We feature both international and domestic travel packages. Our motto is that famous saying, "Take nothing but pictures, leave nothing but footprints."

B. Work with a partner. Discuss the travel agency you read about in activity A. What kinds of letters or symbols would make a good logo for this agency? Write a few ideas below.

_____

_____

C. Write compound, complex, and simple sentences about your design process. Complete the sentences below as a guide.

Green Travel _____, so our logo

design _____.

Our first idea, which _____,

turned out _____.

We chose _____ because

_____.

The most important element of the logo is _____.

D. Draw a sketch of your logo. Try to give your audience an idea of your design. It does not have to be perfect.

E. Write a brief description of the process you and your partner used to design your logo. Use the personal pronoun *we* and a variety of sentences from activity C.

F. Share your description and logo design with the class. As a class, vote on a new logo for Green Travel.

Independent Writing

A. Think of something you would like to create a logo for. It can be a university, school, organization, or company or product you know—or even yourself! Choose something you are already familiar with and write it below.

I will design a logo for _____.

B. Use the word map below to help you brainstorm ideas for the logo.

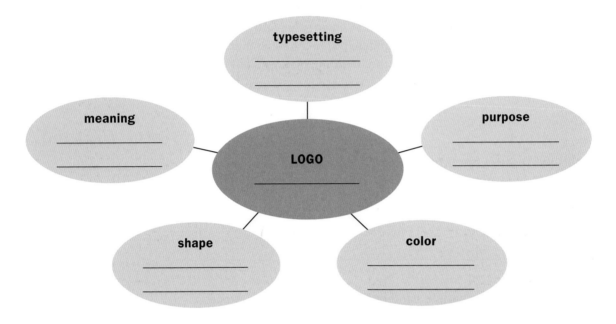

C. What was your thought process while you filled in the chart in activity B? Write five sentences below describing the decisions you made about typesetting, meaning, purpose, color, and shape.

_____

_____

_____

_____

_____

D. Look at the sentences you wrote in activity C. How could you make your sentences more exciting, vivid, and clear to your audience? Edit your sentences in activity C.

VOCABULARY TIP

Use vivid adjectives to help your reader visualize your logo. For example, write *classic* instead of *old* or *bulky* instead of *big*.

E. Sketch a design for your logo in the box below.

(empty box for sketch)

F. Write a draft of your case study. Use your sentences from activity C. Describe what you wanted the logo to represent and why. Explain how your logo meets your requirements. Answer the questions below as a guide for using personal narrative in your case study.

- How many designs did you try before you chose one?
- How did you decide on your final design?
- How did you create your design—on paper, with a computer, in your head?

G. Check your draft for sentence variety. Check both structure and length. Make notes for places where you could change or adjust sentences.

H. Rewrite your case study to include the changes in sentence variety that you noted. Include the target vocabulary from page 125 in your case study. Then sketch a final copy of your logo to include with your case study.

A. Read your case study. Answer the questions below, and make revisions to your case study as needed.

1. Check (✓) the information you included in your case study.

   ☐ elements of the design

   ☐ what the logo is for

   ☐ narrative describing how you chose the design

2. Look at the information you did not include. Would adding that information make your case study more interesting or easier to understand?

Grammar for Editing | Sentence Structure Errors

Check to make sure that simple sentences have a subject and a verb. Some sentences can be very short. Make sure they end with a period.

> **It's not just a word. It's a concept.**

Look for coordinating conjunctions (*and, but, or, yet, for, nor, so*). Place a comma before the conjunction if it links two independent clauses.

> **We have collaborated with other educational institutions on their designs, and we have the experience to help you register your logo and rebrand your image.**

Check that complex sentences contain a dependent clause and an independent clause. The dependent clause begins with a subordinating conjunction and cannot be a sentence on its own.

> **Because the image is abstract, viewers assign their own meanings to the design.**

Use a comma only if the dependent clause is at the beginning of the sentence.

B. Check the language in your case study. Revise and edit as needed.

Language Checklist
☐ I used target words in my case study.
☐ I used a variety of sentence structures.
☐ I used a variety of sentence lengths and types.
☐ I used the correct punctuation.

C. Check your case study again. Repeat activities A and B.

Self-Assessment Review: Go back to page 125 and reassess your knowledge of the target vocabulary. How has your understanding of the words changed? What words do you feel most comfortable using now?

UNIT 10

Mapping Geography's Influence

In this unit, you will

> analyze a persuasive article and learn how it is used on a website.
> use persuasive writing.
> increase your understanding of the target academic words for this unit.

WRITING SKILLS

> Counterarguments
> Supporting a Thesis Statement
> **GRAMMAR** Definite and Indefinite Articles

Self-Assessment

Think about how well you know each target word, and check (✓) the appropriate column. I have…

TARGET WORDS	never seen the word before.	heard or seen the word but am not sure what it means.	heard or seen the word and understand what it means.	used the word confidently in *either* speaking or writing.
AWL				
accumulate				
🔑 civil				
🔑 complex				
compound				
🔑 despite				
🔑 ethnic				
🔑 involve				
likewise				
🔑 nevertheless				
🔑 nuclear				
🔑 overseas				
regime				
🔑 region				
🔑 route				

🔑 Oxford 3000™ keywords

Building Knowledge

Read these questions. Discuss your answers in a small group.

1. How do you think most college and university students decide what to study?

2. Do you think it is better to study a subject that would be useful in many careers, or to study a subject that leads directly to one type of job?

3. What kinds of information, arguments, or reasons could an academic department present that would make you want to study that subject?

Writing Model

A persuasive article uses a mix of information and arguments to convince the reader to think or do something. Read this persuasive article about the importance of geography from a college website.

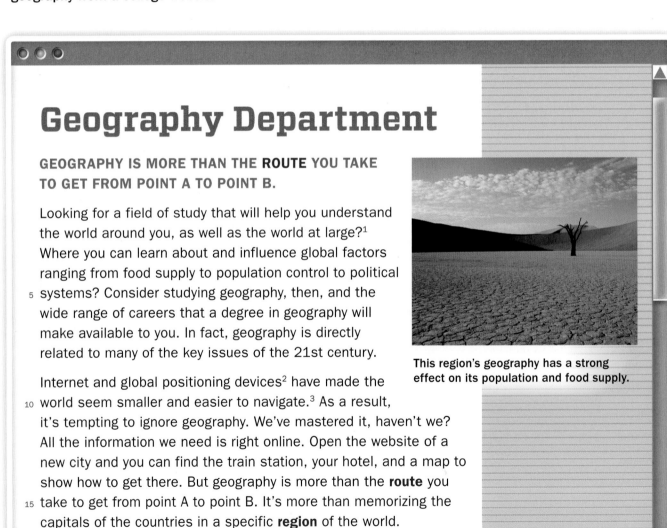

Geography Department

GEOGRAPHY IS MORE THAN THE ROUTE YOU TAKE TO GET FROM POINT A TO POINT B.

Looking for a field of study that will help you understand the world around you, as well as the world at large?[1] Where you can learn about and influence global factors ranging from food supply to population control to political
5 systems? Consider studying geography, then, and the wide range of careers that a degree in geography will make available to you. In fact, geography is directly related to many of the key issues of the 21st century.

Internet and global positioning devices[2] have made the
10 world seem smaller and easier to navigate.[3] As a result, it's tempting to ignore geography. We've mastered it, haven't we? All the information we need is right online. Open the website of a new city and you can find the train station, your hotel, and a map to show how to get there. But geography is more than the **route** you
15 take to get from point A to point B. It's more than memorizing the capitals of the countries in a specific **region** of the world.

This region's geography has a strong effect on its population and food supply.

---

[1] *at large:* in general
[2] *global positioning devices (GPS):* tools that use signals to determine a person's position on Earth
[3] *navigate:* to plan or control a path of travel

THE EARTH SHAPES POLITICS

If you think that studying mountains, rivers, and oceans is only interesting to a tourist, consider the impact that

20 geography can have on politics. It is an important key to understanding the connection between a country's military situation and its political system. It can help explain why some **regimes** stay in

25 power **despite civil** unrest. **Likewise**, it can help explain why some political systems have survived for hundreds of years. An island nation only has to defend itself from attacks from **overseas**. A

30 country surrounded by mountains has natural protection for its borders, just as a **region** with geographically open borders might be frequently conquered—or learn to live in peace with its neighbors.

Geography isn't the only factor **involved** in politics, of course,

35 but physical features can **compound** other issues.

Mountains can prevent armies, but also traders and visitors, from crossing a country's border.

CLIMATE AND ECONOMIC DEVELOPMENT

Study geography and you'll learn how it affects climate, and how climate in turn affects population growth. There's a reason why the ten countries where the fewest people live either have extremely cold climates (such as in Greenland and Iceland) or

40 extremely hot climates (such as in Western Sahara and Mauritania). In addition, climate affects a **region's** economy. It is difficult to farm or harvest enough food in a country covered in sand. It is also difficult to manufacture or produce things to sell there. So is it the weather or the lack of jobs that keeps people

45 from populating these areas?

You might be more interested in solving problems at home than studying international issues. However, geography also determines domestic issues. For instance, experts consider geography to decide where **nuclear** power plants can be located

50 and where new technologies such as wind and solar power can be developed.

The study of geography hasn't always seemed desirable. In the past, people used geography to make incorrect judgments about other people and places. In trying to explain how some nations **accumulate** wealth and others remain poor, geographers and researchers entered into controversial[4] discussions.

These discussions led to incorrect assumptions about **ethnic** and other differences between groups of people. This is part of the reason that some universities closed their geography departments in the late 1940s. But **despite** people using geography to inaccurately judge and label other people, it's a crucial area of study. People nowadays understand more about the **complexity** of factors that influence human behavior.

Energy use, sustainable agriculture, political instability, and access to water are examples of modern issues related to geography. There are particular advantages and disadvantages to a place, and finding a solution to the problems in an area requires an understanding of that place's geography.

Discussing the factors, issues, and problems associated with geography is challenging and sometimes controversial. Nevertheless, it's a conversation we must have. It can lead to a greater understanding of the world we live in. Geography affects a place's culture—what you wear, eat, believe, and do—its political systems, and its economy. Geography affects life. Can there be a more complex or important field of study?

Students with a wide range of interests will find what they want in the Geography Department.

[4] *controversial*: describes something that people are likely to disagree about

WRITING SKILL Counterarguments

LEARN

When writing a persuasive text, consider the arguments against your opinion or position. If your readers are likely to be aware of these arguments, you can write about them. This gives you the opportunity to argue against them. This technique is known as introducing a counterargument—an argument against your position.

To use this persuasive strategy, state the counterargument first. Then explain why your position is more valid, important, or reasonable.

Consider these questions to help you respond to the counterargument:

1. Is the counterargument untrue? If so, how can you show or prove this?

2. Is the counterargument unimportant? What more important points can you bring up to support your position?

3. Does the counterargument point out a problem that can easily be solved? If so, explain the solution.

Use phrases such as these to introduce and respond to a counterargument:

To introduce a counterargument	To answer a counterargument
Some people believe / say / claim that…	However… / But…
It has been argued / said that…	If…then… / Even if…
It might seem that…	Nevertheless…

APPLY

A. Read the persuasive article on pages 142–144 again. Check (✓) the counterarguments against majoring in geography that the writer mentions in the article.

_____ a. It's a very difficult subject, and many students fail their classes.

_✓_ b. People don't think it's necessary to study geography now because directions are easy to find online.

_____ c. If you get a degree in geography, it can be difficult to find a job.

_____ d. Geography is interesting, but many other majors are more interesting.

_____ e. Studying the shape of Earth is interesting, but it isn't important.

_____ f. Geography is only relevant to people who want to travel.

_____ g. It's difficult to register for geography classes because they fill up quickly.

_____ h. Geography was an unpopular subject in the past because people used it to justify thoughts and actions that were harmful others.

_____ i. Geography classes are usually offered at the most popular times during the day, so it's hard to take other required classes at the same time.

_____ j. It's difficult to discuss and understand geography because there aren't clear answers.

B. Write the letter of the counterargument from activity A that matches the writer's response in the persuasive article.

_f_ 1. Geography affects local issues, too.

___ 2. Even if it's difficult to understand, it's important to study and discuss.

___ 3. Geography also affects important issues like politics and climate.

___ 4. Geography is a more complex subject than just the study of maps.

___ 5. Even if it was misused before, it's important to study geography today.

Analyze

A. The underlined transition phrases show the relationship between the sentences in each pair below. Write the letter that names the relationship for each pair. You may use some letters more than once.

A = Comparison   B = Contrast   C = Example   D = Explanation

_D_ 1. Internet and global positioning devices have made the world seem smaller and easier to navigate. <u>As a result</u>, it's tempting to ignore geography.

___ 2. Open a new city's website and you can find a map to show you how to get around. <u>But</u> geography is more than the route you take to get from point A to B.

___ 3. Geography can help explain why some regimes stay in power despite civil unrest. <u>Likewise</u>, it can help explain why some political systems have survived for hundreds of years.

___ 4. There's a reason why the ten countries where the fewest people live either have extremely cold or extremely hot climates. <u>In addition</u>, climate affects a region's economy.

___ 5. But geography also determines domestic issues. <u>For instance</u>, experts consider geography to decide where nuclear power plants can be located and where new technologies such as wind and solar power can be developed.

___ 6. But <u>despite</u> people using geography to inaccurately judge and label other people, it's a crucial area of study.

B. Discuss these questions with the class.

1. What do you think is the author's strongest argument for studying geography? Why might an author place the strongest argument near the end of a text?

2. Can you think of any other counterarguments (arguments against majoring in geography)? How could the writer respond to those counterarguments?

C. The author connects geography to several other fields of study. After reading the article, do you feel that geography is more related to your interests than you had realized? Write your response below. Share your answer with a partner.

_____

_____

Vocabulary Activities | STEP I: Word Level

A. Read this excerpt from a lecture about geography. In each sentence, circle the word or phrase in parentheses ( ) that has the same meaning as the underlined word. Compare your answers with a partner.

Throughout the world there are geographical <u>regions</u> ((areas), provinces, regimes) that include parts of more than one country. For example, the Basque region includes part of both France and Spain. <u>Likewise</u> (Although, Exceptionally, Similarly), Patagonia is a region shared by Chile and Argentina. The people living within regions such as these often speak the same language and are the same <u>ethnicity</u> (civilian, culture and race, nuclear family). Some of these people have a <u>complex</u> (complicated, mutual, cultural) relationship with the country in which their part of the region is located. <u>Nonetheless</u> (Anyway, Because, Usually), regions and nations must be <u>involved</u> (accompanied, connected, moved) with each other in order to coexist.

A *regime* is "a method or system of government, especially one that has not been elected in a fair way."

World leaders expressed disappointment at the action taken by the **regime**.

A *regimen* is "a set of actions that you repeat regularly in order to achieve a goal."

Marta's fitness **regimen** *includes stretching, running, and weight training.*

 CORPUS

B. Read the following descriptions. Does each one describe a regime, a regimen, or neither? Write the answer.

_____regimen_____ 1. Dr. Patel says to eat lean protein and avoid fatty food.

_____ 2. The ruling party refuses to hold an election despite pressure from civilians.

_____ 3. Leti only exercises once in a while.

_____ 4. The dancers stretch and exercise every day to stay flexible and strong.

C. Write the target word from the box that collocates with the words and phrases below. If the target word is the first word in the collocations, write it at the beginning of the list. Write it at the end of the list if it is the last word in the collocations. Add one more collocate for each word. Use a dictionary for help.

civil	ethnic	nuclear	overseas	route

1. _____nuclear_____ energy, family, physics, weapons, _____reaction_____

2. _____, a direct, a land, an overseas, a scenic _____

3. _____ background, food, group, identity, origin, _____

4. _____ court, rights, servant, war, _____

5. _____, a trip, imported from, traveling _____

Vocabulary Activities STEP II: Sentence Level

D. Write answers to the following questions using the word *accumulate*. Use a dictionary for help.

1. Find the sentence with *accumulate* in the writing model on pages 142–144. According to that sentence, what accumulates what?

   _____A nation_____ accumulates _____.

2. What else might a nation accumulate? _____

3. If you don't clean your house regularly, what might accumulate? _____

   _____

4. What are some ways to accumulate knowledge? _____

   _____

5. What is wrong with the sentence below? How would you rewrite the sentence so that it makes sense? Discuss your ideas with a partner.

   The coffee accumulated sugar.

E. Read the questions about regions. Then write your answers using the word *region*.

1. What region of the world are you from? _____

2. What region of your country do (or did) you live in? _____

3. What is the most popular region of your country to vacation in?

   _____

4. Is there an example of an ethnic region in your country? What is it called?

   _____

F. Rewrite the pairs of sentences below. Use *nevertheless*, *despite*, or *despite the fact that* to show contrast. Use *likewise* to show a similarity. You may combine the sentences in a pair into one sentence or change the order of ideas.

1. The price of the plane ticket I want just went up. I'm still buying it.

   The price of the plane ticket I want just went up. Nevertheless, I'm still buying it.

2. The southwest region is known for its beautiful coastline. The northeast coast is equally scenic.

   _____

3. Most civilians support the new plan. I think it is too expensive.

   _____

4. The region has few job opportunities. Tourism supports a small community of local artists, restaurants, and business owners.

   _____

   _____

In chemistry, a *compound* is "something formed by two or more chemical elements reacting with each other."

   Common salt is a **compound** of one part sodium and one part chloride.

To *compound* something is "to make something bad become even worse."

   The problems were **compounded** by food shortages.
   The snowstorm **compounded** the danger to the lost hikers.

CORPUS

G. Rewrite these sentences with a form of *compound*.

1. Water is a substance that is two parts hydrogen and one part oxygen.

   _____

2. In the southern region, heavy rain made travel difficult. Lightning made the problem worse.

   _____

3. The damage from the rainstorm became worse when flooding caused mudslides on the mountains.

   _____

4. The bottled water ban approved by several towns in the region worsened the financial problems of the bottled water company Aquifi Springs.

   _____

An article comes before or introduces a noun. There are two types of articles: indefinite articles (*a/an*) and the definite article (*the*).

Indefinite Articles for Nonspecific Nouns

Use *a* or *an* before nouns that the reader doesn't know about or that you are introducing for the first time. Also use *a* or *an* for general, nonspecific nouns.

> Picture **a** place. Any place. It could be **a** desert island you've only imagined in your head. (It could be any place or any desert island. It is not a specific one.)

Use *a* before consonant sounds and *an* before vowel sounds.

> There are particular advantages and disadvantages to **a** place, and finding **a** solution to these problems requires **an** understanding of the geographical influences.

No Articles for Plural and Noncount Nonspecific Nouns

Do not use an article if the noun is plural and nonspecific.

> Geographers and researchers have entered into controversial discussions.

Do not use an article if the noun is noncount and nonspecific.

> Cooling hot places is expensive and requires energy.

The Definite Article for Specific Nouns

Use *the* before singular and plural count and noncount nouns you have already introduced.

> A country with access to waterways has an advantage. **The** advantage is that it can trade easily with countries overseas. (*Advantage* was introduced in the first sentence.)

Also use *the* for specific nouns.

> **The** country bordering Haiti is the Dominican Republic. (*Bordering Haiti* defines a specific country.)

	Singular count noun	Plural count noun	Noncount noun
Nonspecific	a/an	no article	no article
Specific	the	the	the

A. Read the paragraph. Then answer the questions on page 151.

World Relief is an international organization that helps settle refugees after they arrive in a new place. Many refugees travel overseas to distant areas of the world far from home. Organizations like World Relief provide services to make this transition easier. All refugees receive an apartment and groceries upon arriving in their new country. Volunteers and counselors from World Relief also provide help with adjusting to the new culture. They assist refugees with job training, language classes, and financial counseling. They also offer medical care and support for those in need.

1. Sentence 1: Why does the indefinite article *an* occur before *international organization*?

   There are many international organizations that help refugees, so

   it is nonspecific.

2. Sentence 1: Why doesn't *refugees* have an article in front of it?

   _____

3. Sentence 2: Why doesn't *overseas* have an article in front of it?

   _____

4. Sentence 4: Why does *apartment* have *an* before it?

   _____

5. Sentence 4: Why doesn't *groceries* have an article in front of it?

   _____

6. Sentence 5: Why does *new culture* have *the* in front of it?

   _____

B. Read the paragraph below. Correct four errors in article use. You may see the wrong article, a missing article, or an article where none is needed.

Do you know where your grandparents grew up? You are probably wondering what answering this question might show. (1) Well, new research shows that if you are able to answer this question, you may be better able to handle the challenges. Knowing your family history affects your sense of self. Specifically, knowing the challenges that your parents and their parents faced can better prepare you to deal with your own problems. Psychologists Dr. Duke and Dr. Fivush discovered that children who knew about their families felt more confident. (2) This helped them face an obstacles. (3) Children were able to see themselves as part of bigger story. (4) They saw themselves as belonging to the family who overcame life's difficulties.

C. Compare your paragraph with a partner. Make any necessary revisions and discuss your answers with the class. What makes each error incorrect?

WRITING SKILL Supporting a Thesis Statement

LEARN

A thesis is a statement or an opinion that writers try to prove is true, usually in an essay or other piece of academic writing. The thesis statement usually appears in the introduction after the main topic has been introduced.

In a persuasive text, the thesis states the writer's main argument. The following paragraphs contain examples, descriptions, and other support for the thesis statement.

1. To write a thesis statement, present your topic first. Then follow it with a position that you will support.

   topic   position
   Where you live determines many important aspects of your life.

2. Support your thesis statement by providing examples and details.

   a. Turn your thesis statement into a question: What important aspects of life are affected by where you live?

   b. Answer your question with statements that you could develop into paragraphs.

   - The job that I get is determined by the types of jobs available in the region where I live.

   - My education is affected by how good the educational system is in my area.

   - My interests and activities are affected by what is available nearby.

APPLY

A. Work with a partner. Identify the thesis statement in the writing model on pages 142–144. Underline the topic and circle the position.

B. Read the ideas below that the author used to support her thesis. With a partner, find one more idea in the writing model that supports the thesis. Write it in the space below.

- Geography can explain why some political systems develop and last.

- Geography affects climate, which has an impact on population growth, business, and the economy.

- Geography impacts energy and technology.

- _____

Collaborative Writing

A. Work with a partner. Imagine that you are reading the sentences below in an essay in favor of land reclamation. Write *A* for the writer's argument, *C* for a counter-argument, and *E* for an example.

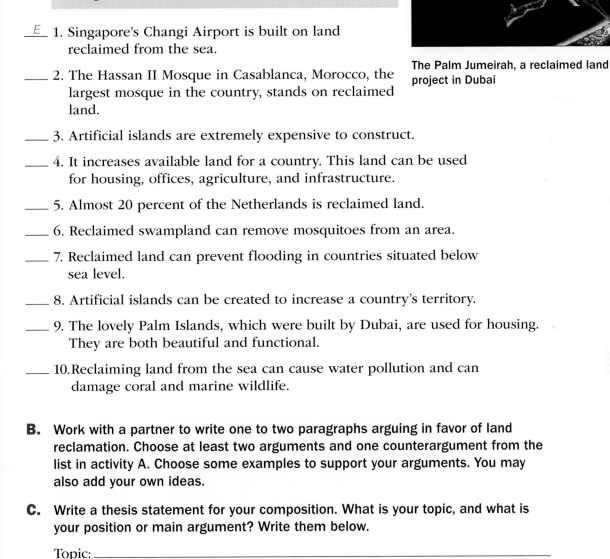

The Palm Jumeirah, a reclaimed land project in Dubai

> Land reclamation is the process of creating new land by adding soil to the shore of an ocean, lake, or river.

_E_ 1. Singapore's Changi Airport is built on land reclaimed from the sea.

____ 2. The Hassan II Mosque in Casablanca, Morocco, the largest mosque in the country, stands on reclaimed land.

____ 3. Artificial islands are extremely expensive to construct.

____ 4. It increases available land for a country. This land can be used for housing, offices, agriculture, and infrastructure.

____ 5. Almost 20 percent of the Netherlands is reclaimed land.

____ 6. Reclaimed swampland can remove mosquitoes from an area.

____ 7. Reclaimed land can prevent flooding in countries situated below sea level.

____ 8. Artificial islands can be created to increase a country's territory.

____ 9. The lovely Palm Islands, which were built by Dubai, are used for housing. They are both beautiful and functional.

____ 10. Reclaiming land from the sea can cause water pollution and can damage coral and marine wildlife.

B. Work with a partner to write one to two paragraphs arguing in favor of land reclamation. Choose at least two arguments and one counterargument from the list in activity A. Choose some examples to support your arguments. You may also add your own ideas.

C. Write a thesis statement for your composition. What is your topic, and what is your position or main argument? Write them below.

Topic: _____

Main argument: _____

D. Now write your persuasive paragraphs. Include your thesis statement, counterargument, arguments, and examples.

E. Compare your paragraphs with another pair. Were your thesis statements similar? How were they different?

Independent Writing

A. You are going to write an article for a college website. You will persuade students of the value of your major field of study or another one that you know about. Choose a field of study to write about.

Field of study: _____

B. Write three arguments to support the position that your field of study is valuable. Order them from least important to most important.

1. _____

2. _____

3. _____

C. Alone or with a partner, brainstorm some counterarguments, or reasons not to study this particular major. Then write your responses to those counterarguments.

Counterarguments
•
•
•

My responses
•
•
•

D. Write your thesis statement. State the topic and provide a position on it that you can argue.

Thesis statement: _____

E. What ideas will you use to support your thesis? Complete the chart below as a guide.

Supporting idea 1:	
Supporting idea 2:	
Supporting idea 3:	

F. Brainstorm examples to develop the arguments in activity E in your supporting paragraphs. Use transition phrases.

Supporting idea 1:	Transition and example:
Supporting idea 2:	Transition and example:
Supporting idea 3:	Transition and example:

> **VOCABULARY TIP**
>
> Use transitions to show the relationship between your sentences. To add further support, details, and examples, use *likewise, in addition, for example, for instance,* and *additionally.*

G. Write a title for your article that is related to your thesis.

_____

H. Write your persuasive article. Use the information from the charts above. In your writing, use target vocabulary words from page 141. Include examples and counterarguments to strengthen your writing. Connect your ideas with appropriate transitions.

REVISE AND EDIT

A. Read your article. Answer the questions below, and make revisions to your article as needed.

1. Check (✓) the information you included in your article.

   ☐ thesis statement

   ☐ supporting arguments

   ☐ counterarguments

   ☐ conclusion that repeats your argument

   ☐ title that connects to your thesis

2. Look at the information you did not include. Would adding that information make your article more persuasive?

Grammar for Editing Common Errors in Article Use

Check that *an* occurs before words that begin with a vowel sound and *a* before consonant sounds. *A* is used before the words below because they begin with a /y/ sound.

> I have to wear ***a*** <u>*uniform*</u> to work. I work at ***a*** <u>*European*</u> bakery.

Use *the* before a specified unit or a period of time, such as *in the morning, in the evening, all the time,* and *most of the time.* However, do not use *the* before *at night* or *at noon.*

> Temperatures today rose above ***the*** <u>predicted 95 degrees Fahrenheit</u>.

B. Check the language in your article. Revise and edit as needed.

Language Checklist
☐ I used target words in my persuasive article.
☐ I introduced counterarguments clearly in my article.
☐ I used definite and indefinite articles appropriately.
☐ I used article forms in my writing correctly.

C. Check your article again. Repeat activities A and B.

Self-Assessment Review: Go back to page 141 and reassess your knowledge of the target vocabulary words. How has your understanding of the words changed? What words do you feel most comfortable using now?

The Academic Word List

Words targeted in Level 3 are bold

Word	Sublist	Location
abandon	8	L2, U6
abstract	**6**	**L3, U1**
academy	5	L2, U8
access	4	L0, U6
accommodate	**9**	**L3, U6**
accompany	8	L4, U6
accumulate	**8**	**L3, U10**
accurate	6	L0, U4
achieve	2	L0, U1
acknowledge	6	L0, U7
acquire	**2**	**L3, U4**
adapt	7	L0, U3
adequate	**4**	**L3, U3**
adjacent	10	L4, U3
adjust	5	L4, U6
administrate	2	L4, U10
adult	7	L0, U8
advocate	7	L4, U4
affect	2	L1, U2
aggregate	6	L4, U5
aid	**7**	**L3, U4**
albeit	10	L4, U9
allocate	**6**	**L3, U1**
alter	5	L2, U6
alternative	3	L1, U7
ambiguous	8	L4, U7
amend	5	L4, U1
analogy	9	L4, U2
analyze	1	L1, U9
annual	4	L1, U6
anticipate	9	L2, U5
apparent	4	L2, U5
append	8	L4, U9
appreciate	8	L0, U8
approach	1	L1, U2
appropriate	**2**	**L3, U4**
approximate	4	L2, U1
arbitrary	8	L4, U7
area	1	L0, U6
aspect	2	L2, U3
assemble	**10**	**L3, U6**
assess	1	L2, U4
assign	**6**	**L3, U9**
assist	2	L0, U4
assume	**1**	**L3, U4**
assure	**9**	**L3, U9**
attach	6	L0, U7

Word	Sublist	Location
attain	**9**	**L3, U5**
attitude	4	L2, U4
attribute	**4**	**L3, U3**
author	6	L0, U9
authority	1	L2, U9
automate	8	L2, U5
available	1	L0, U8
aware	5	L1, U3
behalf	9	L4, U1
benefit	1	L2, U4
bias	8	L4, U2
bond	6	L4, U9
brief	6	L2, U4
bulk	**9**	**L3, U1**
capable	**6**	**L3, U7**
capacity	5	L4, U2
category	2	L2, U3
cease	9	L2, U8
challenge	5	L1, U2
channel	7	L4, U3
chapter	2	L0, U9
chart	8	L0, U8
chemical	7	L2, U10
circumstance	3	L4, U3
cite	6	L4, U7
civil	**4**	**L3, U10**
clarify	**8**	**L3, U8**
classic	**7**	**L3, U9**
clause	**5**	**L3, U3**
code	4	L0, U7
coherent	9	L4, U6
coincide	9	L4, U6
collapse	**10**	**L3, U6**
colleague	**10**	**L3, U1**
commence	9	L2, U9
comment	3	L1, U5
commission	2	L4, U2
commit	4	L2, U2
commodity	8	L4, U10
communicate	4	L1, U3
community	2	L1, U4
compatible	9	L2, U3
compensate	3	L4, U8
compile	**10**	**L3, U2**
complement	8	L4, U9

Oxford 3000™ words

Word	Sublist	Location
🔑 **complex**	2	**L3, U10**
🔑 **component**	3	**L3, U3**
compound	5	**L3, U10**
comprehensive	7	**L3, U3**
comprise	7	**L3, U1**
compute	2	L1, U7
conceive	10	L4, U4
🔑 concentrate	4	L1, U2
🔑 **concept**	1	**L3, U9**
🔑 conclude	2	L0, U2
concurrent	9	L4, U3
🔑 conduct	2	L1, U5
confer	4	L4, U9
confine	9	L4, U4
🔑 confirm	7	L1, U10
🔑 conflict	5	L1, U10
conform	8	**L3, U8**
consent	3	**L3, U7**
consequent	2	L4, U7
🔑 **considerable**	3	**L3, U9**
🔑 consist	1	L1, U1
🔑 constant	3	L1, U7
constitute	1	L4, U1
constrain	3	L4, U5
🔑 construct	2	L2, U1
🔑 consult	5	L2, U2
consume	2	L2, U6
🔑 contact	5	L1, U3
🔑 contemporary	8	L4, U3
🔑 context	1	L2, U4
🔑 **contract**	1	**L3, U4**
contradict	8	L2, U4
contrary	7	**L3, U8**
🔑 **contrast**	4	**L3, U5**
🔑 contribute	3	L1, U4
controversy	9	L2, U1
convene	3	L4, U8
converse	9	L2, U10
🔑 convert	7	L4, U9
🔑 convince	10	L1, U9
cooperate	6	**L3, U2**
coordinate	3	L2, U5
🔑 core	3	L4, U1
corporate	3	L1, U7
correspond	3	**L3, U2**
🔑 couple	7	L0, U7
🔑 create	1	L2, U7
🔑 credit	2	L2, U9
🔑 **criteria**	3	**L3, U3**
🔑 crucial	8	L4, U4
🔑 culture	2	L0, U9
currency	8	L2, U7
🔑 **cycle**	4	**L3, U1**
🔑 data	1	L0, U3
🔑 **debate**	4	**L3, U5**
🔑 decade	7	L1, U9
🔑 decline	5	L1, U6
deduce	3	**L3, U3**
🔑 define	1	L0, U6
🔑 definite	7	L4, U6
🔑 demonstrate	3	L1, U5
denote	8	L4, U10
🔑 deny	7	L1, U10
🔑 depress	10	L0, U10
🔑 derive	1	L4, U2
🔑 design	2	L0, U3
🔑 **despite**	4	**L3, U10**
detect	8	L2, U1
deviate	8	L4, U7
🔑 device	9	L0, U7
🔑 devote	9	L2, U4
differentiate	7	**L3, U8**
dimension	4	L4, U9
diminish	9	L2, U6
discrete	5	L4, U10
discriminate	6	L4, U1
displace	8	**L3, U5**
🔑 display	6	L0, U9
dispose	7	L4, U8
distinct	2	L4, U10
distort	9	L4, U7
🔑 distribute	1	L1, U6
diverse	6	L4, U3
🔑 document	3	L0, U10
domain	6	L4, U7
🔑 domestic	4	L2, U6
🔑 dominate	3	L4, U8
🔑 draft	5	L0, U10
🔑 drama	8	L2, U7
duration	9	L2, U5
dynamic	7	**L3, U1**
🔑 economy	1	L2, U3
edit	6	L1, U1
🔑 **element**	2	**L3, U9**
🔑 eliminate	7	L1, U7
🔑 emerge	4	L4, U10
🔑 emphasis	3	L1, U7
empirical	7	L4, U5
🔑 enable	5	L2, U7
🔑 encounter	10	L1, U5

🔑 Oxford 3000™ words

Word	Sublist	Location
energy	5	L0, U1
enforce	5	L4, U7
enhance	**6**	**L3, U5**
enormous	10	L0, U2
ensure	3	L4, U6
entity	5	L4, U9
environment	1	L1, U6
equate	**2**	**L3, U2**
equip	7	L2, U3
equivalent	5	L1, U10
erode	9	L4, U8
error	4	L0, U4
establish	1	L2, U2
estate	**6**	**L3, U1**
estimate	1	L2, U8
ethic	**9**	**L3, U8**
ethnic	**4**	**L3, U10**
evaluate	2	L1, U8
eventual	**8**	**L3, U5**
evident	1	L2, U1
evolve	5	L2, U8
exceed	6	L1, U8
exclude	3	L2, U2
exhibit	8	L2, U10
expand	5	L0, U2
expert	6	L2, U2
explicit	6	L4, U7
exploit	8	L4, U7
export	**1**	**L3, U9**
expose	5	L4, U8
external	5	L2, U3
extract	**7**	**L3, U5**
facilitate	**5**	**L3, U6**
factor	**1**	**L3, U2**
feature	2	L0, U5
federal	6	L4, U1
fee	6	L0, U5
file	7	L0, U10
final	2	L0, U3
finance	**1**	**L3, U4**
finite	7	L4, U9
flexible	6	L1, U10
fluctuate	8	L4, U6
focus	2	L0, U1
format	9	L2, U1
formula	**1**	**L3, U8**
forthcoming	10	L4, U9
found	9	L0, U10
foundation	7	L1, U9
framework	3	L4, U3

Word	Sublist	Location
function	**1**	**L3, U3**
fund	3	L2, U9
fundamental	5	L1, U8
furthermore	**6**	**L3, U1**
gender	**6**	**L3, U2**
generate	5	L1, U4
generation	5	L2, U8
globe	7	L2, U1
goal	4	L0, U1
grade	7	L0, U9
grant	**4**	**L3, U2**
guarantee	7	L1, U4
guideline	8	L1, U8
hence	**4**	**L3, U1**
hierarchy	7	L4, U10
highlight	8	L0, U7
hypothesis	**4**	**L3, U7**
identical	**7**	**L3, U7**
identify	1	L1, U5
ideology	7	L4, U3
ignorance	6	L2, U10
illustrate	3	L0, U6
image	5	L1, U7
immigrate	3	L4, U8
impact	2	L2, U6
implement	4	L4, U7
implicate	**4**	**L3, U7**
implicit	8	L4, U1
imply	**3**	**L3, U5**
impose	**4**	**L3, U8**
incentive	6	L4, U5
incidence	**6**	**L3, U2**
incline	10	L4, U6
income	**1**	**L3, U2**
incorporate	6	L4, U3
index	6	L4, U8
indicate	1	L2, U3
individual	1	L0, U4
induce	8	L4, U4
inevitable	8	L4, U1
infer	7	L4, U2
infrastructure	8	L4, U10
inherent	9	L4, U5
inhibit	6	L4, U5
initial	3	L0, U4
initiate	**6**	**L3, U2**
injure	2	L4, U6
innovate	**7**	**L3, U3**

Word	Sublist	Location		Word	Sublist	Location
input	6	L2, U2		maximize	3	L1, U7
insert	7	L2, U7		**mechanism**	**4**	**L3, U3**
insight	**9**	**L3, U7**		media	7	L0, U9
inspect	8	L4, U7		**mediate**	**9**	**L3, U4**
instance	**3**	**L3, U4**		medical	5	L1, U2
institute	2	L1, U8		medium	9	L1, U10
instruct	6	L1, U10		mental	5	L2, U10
integral	9	L4, U5		method	1	L1, U3
integrate	4	L4, U7		migrate	6	L4, U10
integrity	10	L2, U8		military	9	L2, U9
intelligence	6	L0, U8		minimal	9	L1, U8
intense	**8**	**L3, U7**		**minimize**	**8**	**L3, U9**
interact	3	L2, U1		minimum	6	L1, U8
intermediate	9	L2, U7		ministry	6	L4, U1
internal	4	L1, U2		minor	3	L0, U8
interpret	1	L4, U2		**mode**	**7**	**L3, U2**
interval	**6**	**L3, U7**		modify	5	L1, U10
intervene	**7**	**L3, U4**		**monitor**	**5**	**L3, U7**
intrinsic	10	L4, U5		motive	6	L2, U4
invest	**2**	**L3, U9**		mutual	9	L2, U10
investigate	4	L2, U9				
invoke	10	L4, U9		negate	3	L4, U8
involve	**1**	**L3, U10**		network	5	L2, U5
isolate	**7**	**L3, U4**		neutral	6	L2, U9
issue	1	L0, U6		**nevertheless**	**6**	**L3, U10**
item	2	L0, U5		nonetheless	10	L4, U6
				norm	9	L4, U5
job	4	L0, U3		normal	2	L0, U3
journal	2	L1, U9		notion	5	L4, U2
justify	**3**	**L3, U2**		notwithstanding	10	L4, U2
				nuclear	**8**	**L3, U10**
label	4	L0, U5				
labor	1	L2, U4		objective	5	L0, U4
layer	3	L4, U10		**obtain**	**2**	**L3, U1**
lecture	6	L0, U8		obvious	4	L1, U5
legal	1	L1, U3		occupy	4	L4, U6
legislate	1	L4, U1		occur	1	L2, U1
levy	10	L4, U4		odd	10	L1, U1
liberal	5	L4, U3		**offset**	**8**	**L3, U2**
license	**5**	**L3, U6**		ongoing	10	L2, U5
likewise	**10**	**L3, U10**		option	4	L1, U9
link	3	L0, U5		orient	5	L4, U7
locate	3	L1, U1		outcome	3	L2, U4
logic	**5**	**L3, U1**		output	4	L2, U3
				overall	4	L2, U3
maintain	2	L1, U4		overlap	9	L2, U9
major	1	L0, U2		**overseas**	**6**	**L3, U10**
manipulate	8	L4, U2				
manual	**9**	**L3, U3**		panel	10	L4, U1
margin	5	L2, U4		paradigm	7	L4, U9
mature	9	L2, U8		paragraph	8	L1, U1

Word	Sublist	Location	Word	Sublist	Location
parallel	4	L4, U10	radical	8	L4, U2
parameter	**4**	**L3, U8**	random	8	L2, U10
participate	2	L1, U1	range	2	L2, U3
partner	3	L0, U5	**ratio**	**5**	**L3, U6**
passive	**9**	**L3, U8**	**rational**	**6**	**L3, U8**
perceive	2	L4, U6	react	3	L1, U5
percent	1	L1, U7	recover	6	L2, U5
period	**1**	**L3, U4**	**refine**	**9**	**L3, U1**
persist	**10**	**L3, U7**	**regime**	**4**	**L3, U10**
perspective	5	L2, U3	**region**	**2**	**L3, U10**
phase	4	L2, U1	**register**	**3**	**L3, U9**
phenomenon	7	L4, U5	**regulate**	**2**	**L3, U3**
philosophy	**3**	**L3, U9**	**reinforce**	**8**	**L3, U6**
physical	3	L0, U1	reject	5	L1, U10
plus	8	L0, U6	relax	9	L0, U4
policy	1	L2, U8	release	7	L1, U6
portion	9	L2, U6	**relevant**	**2**	**L3, U2**
pose	10	L4, U2	reluctance	10	L2, U8
positive	2	L0, U1	rely	3	L2, U6
potential	2	L2, U5	remove	3	L0, U8
practitioner	8	L4, U4	require	1	L0, U3
precede	**6**	**L3, U8**	research	1	L0, U2
precise	**5**	**L3, U9**	reside	2	L4, U4
predict	4	L0, U3	resolve	4	L2, U4
predominant	8	L4, U10	resource	2	L0, U4
preliminary	9	L2, U5	respond	1	L1, U4
presume	6	L4, U6	restore	8	L2, U5
previous	2	L0, U5	**restrain**	**9**	**L3, U6**
primary	2	L1, U4	restrict	2	L2, U6
prime	5	L4, U6	retain	4	L4, U8
principal	4	L2, U7	reveal	6	L2, U10
principle	**1**	**L3, U8**	**revenue**	**5**	**L3, U9**
prior	4	L2, U9	**reverse**	**7**	**L3, U4**
priority	7	L2, U5	revise	8	L1, U8
proceed	1	L2, U7	revolution	9	L4, U3
process	1	L1, U5	rigid	9	L2, U8
professional	4	L1, U8	role	1	L0, U7
prohibit	**7**	**L3, U5**	**route**	**9**	**L3, U10**
project	4	L1, U1			
promote	4	L4, U4	scenario	9	L2, U8
proportion	3	L2, U6	schedule	7	L1, U2
prospect	8	L4, U2	scheme	3	L4, U8
protocol	9	L4, U8	scope	6	L2, U10
psychology	5	L2, U6	section	1	L0, U2
publication	**7**	**L3, U7**	sector	1	L4, U9
publish	3	L0, U10	secure	2	L1, U4
purchase	2	L0, U5	seek	2	L2, U9
pursue	5	L4, U1	select	2	L1, U6
			sequence	3	L1, U6
qualitative	9	L4, U5	series	4	L0, U2
quote	7	L1, U9	sex	3	L4, U5

Oxford 3000™ words

Word	Sublist	Location
shift	3	L2, U7
significant	**1**	**L3, U7**
similar	1	L1, U6
simulate	**7**	**L3, U3**
site	2	L1, U1
so-called	10	L2, U1
sole	7	L4, U4
somewhat	**7**	**L3, U5**
source	1	L1, U6
specific	1	L1, U3
specify	3	L1, U9
sphere	9	L4, U2
stable	**5**	**L3, U6**
statistic	4	L2, U10
status	4	L0, U9
straightforward	**10**	**L3, U3**
strategy	2	L2, U2
stress	4	L0, U1
structure	1	L2, U7
style	5	L2, U2
submit	7	L1, U10
subordinate	9	L4, U9
subsequent	**4**	**L3, U5**
subsidy	6	L4, U3
substitute	5	L2, U6
successor	**7**	**L3, U8**
sufficient	3	L4, U1
sum	**4**	**L3, U5**
summary	4	L1, U3
supplement	9	L2, U10
survey	2	L2, U9
survive	7	L2, U8
suspend	9	L4, U1
sustain	**5**	**L3, U6**
symbol	5	L0, U10
tape	6	**L3, U5**
target	5	L2, U2
task	3	L0, U6
team	9	L0, U1
technical	**3**	**L3, U6**
technique	**3**	**L3, U6**
technology	3	L2, U3
temporary	9	L0, U6
tense	7	L2, U1
terminate	7	L4, U8
text	2	L0, U10
theme	7	L1, U9
theory	**1**	**L3, U7**
thereby	7	L4, U6
thesis	**7**	**L3, U7**

Word	Sublist	Location
topic	7	L0, U7
trace	6	L4, U10
tradition	2	L0, U9
transfer	2	L1, U6
transform	**6**	**L3, U1**
transit	5	L2, U2
transmit	7	L4, U10
transport	6	L1, U8
trend	5	L1, U3
trigger	9	L4, U4
ultimate	**7**	**L3, U9**
undergo	10	L4, U4
underlie	6	L4, U5
undertake	4	L4, U3
uniform	7	L2, U10
unify	9	L2, U9
unique	7	L2, U7
utilize	**6**	**L3, U6**
valid	**3**	**L3, U8**
vary	1	L1, U2
vehicle	7	L2, U2
version	5	L1, U9
via	7	L4, U3
violate	**9**	**L3, U6**
virtual	**8**	**L3, U5**
visible	7	L0, U2
vision	9	L2, U2
visual	8	L2, U7
volume	3	L1, U7
voluntary	**7**	**L3, U4**
welfare	5	L4, U4
whereas	5	L4, U5
whereby	10	L4, U8
widespread	**7**	**L3, U4**